# The Rage
Reflections
on Risk

*This book is dedicated to Ferdinand and Ruth De Maio,
my loving father and mother, who have supported me,
unquestioned, in all my various incarnations.*

*To be sure, it was never easy for them to watch me,
their youngest child, invest his life-force in such dangerous exploits in the vein of "following my passion
and tapping into my primal instincts." They provided
me with a solid foundation from which to nurture,
reach and realize my aptitude in an arena where the
"why?" was, at times, difficult for them to fathom
— yet the stakes very clearly understood.*

Steve De Maio

# THE RAGE

## Reflections on Risk

*Steve DeMaio*

Rocky
Mountain Books
Calgary–Victoria–Vancouver

Rocky Mountain Books
#108 – 17665 66A Avenue
Surrey, BC V3S 2A7
www.rmbooks.com

**Library and Archives Canada Cataloguing in Publication**

De Maio, Steve, 1964-
    The Rage : Reflections on Risk / Steve De Maio.

ISBN 1-894765-63-X

1. De Maio, Steve, 1964- 2. Risk-taking (Psychology).
3. Risk-taking (Psychology)--Poetry. I. Title.

BF637.R57D44 2005          158.1          C2005-904022-X

Edited by Gillean Daffern
Book design by Gillean Daffern
Cover design by Gillean Daffern

Front cover photo: Steve De Maio on the last pitch of Highlander, Yamnuska. Photo Tom Walker.
Back cover photo: Steve De Maio at the fifth belay, Iron Butterfly on the north face of Windtower. Photo Jeff Marshall.
Photo on page 176: Steve De Maio. Photo Gerry De Maio.

Printed in Canada

Rocky Mountain Books acknowledges the financial support for its publishing program from the Government of Canada through the Book Publishing Industry Development Program (BPIDP).

This book has been produced on 100% post-consumer paper, processed chlorine free and printed with vegetable-based inks.

# Contents

# Foreword by Chic Scott

For most of humanity the goal is to create a cocoon of comfort and security. But for a few among us, like Steve De Maio, the drive is towards danger, pain and difficulty on the ragged edge of what is possible. It is a place for a rock climber, where one's life hangs in the balance and with even a small mistake is forfeit.

Like Steve, I too have played this crazy but addicting game, although not with the same commitment. I struggled with the mundane and seemingly meaningless round of school, jobs, girls and careers. Like Steve I hungered for the weekends — to be high on some windy crag with the ravens, where I felt truly alive and there seemed some point to it all.

I first met Steve in 1986. At the time I was in a tranquil backwater of my life, resting and gathering strength. Steve, however, was filled with a passion that I could understand. Often he came to me for encouragement and I hope I helped him to follow his dreams. Steve went on to complete some of the most extreme climbs in the Canadian Rockies and to satisfy the fire that burned within.

The fire never goes out entirely. That is a fact that I know from my own personal experience. Like an old warhorse smelling the gunpowder and hearing the cannon, we continue to dream of further adventures. But the chance never comes again, at least not in the same way. If you don't heed the call the first time round it is gone.

Steve did heed the call and lived to write about it. In this book you will share his rock climbing adventures on Yamnuska and read, with sweaty palms, of his misadventures kayaking the White Salmon River. And there is heartbreaking tragedy when Brian Wallace falls and dies. Through all of this Steve examines his need to push to the psycho-physical edge. You may not understand his passion or want to emulate it, but you must admire it, for it is the same spirit that led the explorers across the oceans, to the poles and later to the moon. Without it humankind is a much-diminished creation.

Steve's passion is a cry to live life fully and unafraid at the border of the possible, whether it is climbing, kayaking, snowboarding or in business. It is a passion that we are in need of even more than ever in our comfortable and risk-averse society. Like Ulysses, Steve can say that he has, "drunk delight of battle with my peers, far on the ringing plains of windy Troy."

Slightly different versions of the following stories were first published
in the following magazines and journals:

Highlander *CAJ, 1988.*
The Boulevard *CAJ, 1989.*
The Obsession *Explore Magazine, Sept/Oct 1988.*
Jimmy and the Kid *CAJ, 1990.* Republished in *The Canadian Anthology of Mountaineering, 1994.* Awarded the Canadian Himalayan Foundation writing prize.
The Psycho/Physical Edge *CAJ 1993.*
The Rage *CAJ 1994.*
The East End Boys *CAJ 1998* (Article of the Year).
Surfin' the Curve *CAJ 2000.*

# The Hard Years
## 1985-1990

These were the harvest years when the investment of time, emotional and physical energy created some of the most serious and demanding climbs of my climbing career. This period culminated with the death of a climbing partner.

# Highlander

I drove hunched over the wheel, still chilled with the morning dampness. I was alone, a rebel, but with a cause and a desire to test myself. There was a burning in my chest. My mind raced with mental preparation: Did I have everything? Rack, two ropes, jugs, water, boots, food, extra clothes, flashlight … I think so.

While hiking up the trail I went over each step of my self-belay technique. I was interrupted at the base of Yam by some army lads who asked me what route I had planned. I felt I couldn't tell them "I am going to try to rope-solo a new line left of Direttisima," as I already had fears of my own which didn't need any re-enforcement.

My intended line followed the first two pitches of Direttisima before moving left onto new ground. I found these pitches gripping. The rock seemed greasy and I couldn't help thinking, "This is only 5.8?" I really believe that the definition of a classic climb should be "an easy climb that scares the shit out of you!"

The second I stepped off Direttisima and onto new ground, my whole body relaxed. I now had no preconception of what lay ahead. I just took it as it came.

This pitch climbed over some suspect blocks to a hanging belay in a huge corner below an overhanging and flaring groove. Time for the etriers! For the next 80 feet I aided and free climbed up this groove. The rope swept down through the runners in a slow arc to the belay station without once touching the rock. In the last 80 feet it overhung 15 feet! The protection was brilliant and I felt very secure. This was the kind of climbing I'd dreamed about: Committed yet in control; pushing myself, yet relaxed. My spine tingled as it did when I read of such greats as Layton Kor and Joe Brown. I felt as though all the karma of past experiences and climbs had come together and was surging out of my fingertips and into the focus of this attempt.

Rappelling the pitch to clean it was good value in itself. Swinging in and out, I tried not to think about all those little edges …

I began a 160 foot traverse to the left. It was steep and never obvious what was going to be the easiest way. I knocked off some loose rock which set off yells from the army lads below. But they were hundreds of feet away and I had work to do, so I threw more rocks off and continued climbing. I felt very alone and insignificant on this part of the wall. It was now 5:00 p.m. and I was only just over half way. I thought, "I'm pushing the envelope a bit here," and decided that if the corner above looked evil I'd traverse back and rap off. When I finally could see around into the corner, I saw a beautiful and relatively low-angled dihedral running right to the top. "OOOOEEE SON!!!"

Rappelling and jugging the traverse was a fairly complex fiasco. After lowering out off the belay and negotiating two more pendulums on my way back left I thought, "Man, if I was someone else up here, he might not know how to do this!" At that moment, I was glad it was me.

Right off of the next belay was a scary run out through a looseish bulge. I tried to imagine myself as Bjorn Borg the Ice Man, calm and cool. I couldn't afford to get excited here. I climbed like a machine: "Test handhold, place hand, move. Tap hold with foot, place foot, look and move." The belay system is more complex than usual while rope-soloing. Any error in any link could have "not fun" consequences. I had a system and I stuck to it.

The climbing up the corner was beautiful: Solid rock and incut holds. I had run out the second pitch up the corner and was only 60 feet from the top when I noticed the light was fading. I didn't want to set up another belay point so I tied on the other rope and kept climbing.

Six feet from the top I was blocked by a two-foot bulging overhang. I had a shitty Friend in a flare, and a knife blade and a wire behind a suspect block. My next piece was 40 feet below (an intermediate piece had been pulled out by the rope). I tried to the left and the right. I felt like a trapped squirrel. I hung there in the fading light thinking, "I just need an edge to sink my meat-hooks into."

I made an irreversible stretch and my fingers sunk into an incut jug on the lip. I brought my other hand up — thank Christ there was room for it — and thought of what a friend had said only weeks before: "You always climb your best when you have to!"

"Well, here goes." I brought my feet up on some slopers and reached up and left for a hold.

"Climb as if on eggshells. That's it! No, uh?"

I pulled off a block and not wanting to be put off balance throwing it off, I pushed it back onto the wall. "A bit further left, yes, not too hard on it now."

I made one more move and was on top.

"Fuck me. I pulled it off … " I almost couldn't believe I was there — on top. I wouldn't let myself relax, I still had to get the gear. I rapped down, being careful not to blow it passing the knot, and was shortly back on top, away from the abyss, devouring a box of Fig Newtons.

# Highlander

Six feet
from the top, blocked
by a two-foot bulge.
The sun is down,
all I have is twilight.
A shitty friend in a flare,
a knife blade and wire
behind a hollow block.

Trapped.
I've tried to the left
I've tried to the right.
Feel like a trapped squirrel
stranded in the fading light.
Seventeen hours of toil
brought me neatly
to this moment.

Hesitate
And be benighted.
The toys are crap.
It's impossible to rap.
Lucky if I can
downclimb
To that ledge below.

Rush
and take a screamer.
Pray my rope-solo
system holds the fall.
Smashing a femur
is good if its
the only consequence.

Irreversibly
I stretch. My meat hooks
grapple a small edge.
Got to match on it,
pad feet on slopers.
I'm committed.
You climb your best
when you have to.

Reach up
and left gently now …
Climb as if on eggshells.
A block pulls
away in my hand.
Push it back on the wall.
A bit further left and
not too hard on it now.

Finally
one more move
and I'm on top.
Fuck me! I pulled it off.
Like a blind man
I feel my way
down the backside
And begin anew.

# The Boulevard

It was 5:00 a.m. Kelly had slept in. I didn't have his phone number. I didn't know where he lived. I was on fire, raging with energy and enthusiasm. I had enough gear to make an attempt alone. The decision was made: "Rock and Roll!"

I jumped in the car and headed for the Bow Corridor. I'd always considered myself to be a man of action and intensity. Internal fires often raged within me. It was rarely a question of wanting to go climbing, it was a question of having to go. Climbing was the "Grand Outlet." I'd found nothing else like it. It could absorb all I could give and usually succeeded in quieting the flames. Otherwise it's like trying to fight a roaring inferno with a two by four: It doesn't work! So ... "Climb Man! Climb! Climb like a Beast!"

It was still dark when I arrived at the trail head. Earphones in place, I began the hump up Exshaw Creek to the base of the south face of Mount Fable.

Once out of the trees and onto the grass and rock slopes below the face, I was buffeted by the wind. It blew me onto my knees several times, my pack seeming to act as a sail.

I'd brought with me bivy gear, two ropes, a huge rack, a 2.2 kg. tin of peanut butter, 750 ml of jam, 12 pita pockets, and for entertainment, my Walkman and camera — the whole nine yards. It wasn't long before my batteries ran out and I hit the auto-rewind button on my camera. Superfluous weight? No way! Good Training! For what I'm not sure. The trip seemed doomed from the start.

I climbed up the slabs below the main face as far as I dared with my pig of a pack on my back. I pounded in a multi-piton belay and clipped off the pack. Aah ... Fun, sun and fires ... I chuckled to myself, "you rock hound, you!" I was excited.

Two hundred and fifty feet above I could see a large cave. It looked tricky getting up to and around the cave, but above that it appeared I could follow a system of ramps through otherwise vertical or overhanging rock. I chortled "nuk, nuk, nuk" and was off.

To get up to the cave I was forced to climb a short steep section of semi-rotten rock. Thankfully I was following a crack and was able to lace it with pins and tap a few wires in. I kept looking ahead, back at my pro and down at the talus, "Hmmm … not a good place to fall here, lad."

Pretty soon I was on easier ground — a full rope length run out. To save time, I tied the 9 mm rope to the 11 mm rope, put in a re-belay and continued climbing. I knew I probably shouldn't do this, but I figured, "Nobody will know." And anyway, it didn't look too bad.

One hundred and fifty feet later I reached the cave. I could not have asked for a better camp site, or so I thought at the time. I rapped down to clean the pitch, retrieve the "pig" and take apart the belay. In the belay I'd used a home-made piton I was testing for a friend. I bashed the head back and forth a few times. It moved quite easily.

"That's funny … I thought it was a better placement than that."

I stuck the pick of my hammer into the eye and pulled. It came out easily enough except I now had only the eye of the piton on the end of my hammer. The rest of the pin was still in the crack!

I managed to fix two more pitches above the cave before nightfall and then rapped back down to the cave where I devoured my quota of peanut butter and jam pitas and then tried to sleep.

The wind howled outside. I thought briefly about the ropes. Nah, I had tied them down drum tight.

I drifted off only to become vaguely aware of a disturbing scratching sound. I lay there listening, then suddenly realized what it must be.

"You little bastard!!"

I grabbed my headlamp and shone it towards where the rope was anchored. There he was, those little beady eyes staring back at me. I imagined a little rat-tongue sticking out and squeaking, "You can't get me! You can't get me!" in a taunting chant. I launched a rock in his direction and missed, but it seemed to do the trick. Back to sleep …

I started awake. There was a weight on my legs and a scratching on my sleeping bag!! I shrieked and catapulted my legs into the air. The little bugger must have flown because my toes sure became acquainted with the roof of the cave. I lay there in agony, cursing and waiting for the throbbing in my toes to stop.

By morning I was almost praying for rain. I poked one eye out of my sleeping bag. A little Troll whispered into my ear, as though perched on my left shoulder, "Clouds in the Bow Corridor, you know what that means: Time to go down."

teve, you know those clouds
you don't go climbing because
ing."

eciding to sleep another hour and
o bright sunlight and no Trolls. Go!
e ropes!

the 11 mm rope had been cut through
ht.

"I. d from nowhere. "Go for it man! You've
got the ᵗ e fuss about? You're not going to wank out
are you?"

Then from the ᵗ her side: "Fuck off, we're not wanking out, this
is a mountaineering judgment."

Again I settled it. It would be silly to carry on. It's funny how
when in a serious position you often imagine what the headlines
might be: "Climber Killed ... appears he continued climbing with
chopped ropes."

It had a sobering effect.

I would be rappelling to the right of the line I had climbed and into
unknown terrain. The first few raps went well. Then I pounded in
another two piton station and began pulling on the 9 mm. It moved
eight feet and stopped. The sirens went off. The loudspeaker in my
brain screamed "battle stations." I tried everything. The rope would
not budge in either direction. Back up the ropes I went. I managed
to unhook them and began to make my way back down when the
sheath of the 11 mm rope, which was now completely cut all the way
around, bunched up and jammed in my Sticht plate. I eventually
managed to unweight the device and worry the rope through.

The rope pulled OK until the knot was 20 feet above me, then it
jammed again. This time I knew it was the sheath jamming in the
rappel sling at the station. The other end of the rope may as well
have been in the ozone layer and I refused to jug up on a rope sheath
with no backup. But there was the knot, only 20 feet above.

The Trolls were back. "Cut the rope and rap from here, you can
make it. Bill won't mind 20 feet off of his rope," and the other: "Clip
the rope off, give yourself 20 feet of slack and climb up to and untie
the knot."

Hmmm ... This time I wasn't sure who was who. I could not afford to buy Bill a new rope and the terrain looked moderate. So I
climbed up and untied the knot with one hand and my teeth, then
downclimbed back to the belay. It was one 80 foot rap to the scree
and I was away into the valley.

"You wanked out!"

"I did not!"

"Good judgment, Steve."

I knew I'd done the right thing. I also knew I'd be back.

It was five months later. I hadn't initially planned another solo attempt on Fable that day. I had planned to try a new aid line on Yam. My partner showed up at our meeting place at 5:00 a.m. but with news of an injured knee. I had not enough gear with my own personal rack for the proposed route, but I had enough enthusiasm for five routes! My mind raced. Fable! Fable! Fable! Did I have enough gear? Just ...

All winter I'd thought about the errors I'd made on my last attempt. Apart from trying to solo it, I'd taken way too much gear. This time I'd take no bivy gear, a single 10 mm rope and a 6 mm rap cord. I'd take only a light rack, only a few extra clothes and no camera or Walkman. For food I would take only three chocolate bars.

I stormed up the trail. There was still snow on much of the slope below the face.

This time I could solo higher up the initial slabs with the lighter pack. I had about seven feet to go to a niche where I wanted to set up my first stance. The sequence proved too difficult with the pack on.

The Trolls were back. "Go for it man! Think of the time you'll save!"

"No, Steve, set up a stance here and do it properly You know what you always say: 'Fuck around, fuck around. Pretty soon you won't be around.'"

"Fuck the both of you!! I'll make up my own mind!"

I took the pack off and balanced it on a small ledge. Then I carefully uncoiled the rope and tied one end to the pack. With the other end in my teeth, I made the move into the niche and set up the stance. If the pack slipped off the ledge while I was making the move, I didn't want to be tied to it.

I rocked up the first four pitches past the cave to the high point. Passing the trashed 11 mm now strewn across the rock below was a bit unnerving. I tried not to let it bother me.

Another rope length brought me to a large ledge. I knew this ledge marked the half-way point on the face. While jugging the pitch my forearms began cramping up on me. I'd been going for eight or nine hours from the trailhead non-stop. I broke out a chocolate bar and took off my rock shoes. The sun was out and there was not a breath of wind. I revelled in the moment. I could have a nap right there ...

Then the voice: "Get moving! This isn't a union job!" The voice was right.

The rock directly above looked evil, but I spied a corner 20 feet down and 60 feet to the left at the other end of a ledge. The Trolls were arguing among themselves about my route finding. I took no heed. If there was one thing I had learned it was to take the line of least resistance.

Thus far the line had followed a surprisingly moderate system of ramps back and forth across the face. When I stepped across into the corner I was amazed at the void below my feet. It seemed the crag was pretty much vertical and these ramps made their way up the face in much the same way as a fire escape does on the side of a tall building.

I fought my way up the right-leaning, gently-impending corner. There was a good crack with good finger locks and jams.

"Just aid it, no one will know."

"Shut up, will you! I'm pumped!"

I put a Friend in and grabbed the sling so I could clip the rope in more easily.

"Uh! I saw that ... it's not free now!"

I didn't care. Survival came first.

I pulled onto a stance. There was very little for a belay. Time for a bolt. The next pitch looked fierce. A rail ran up an otherwise blank wall at an angle of 70 degrees. On any other kind of rock, there would have been a crack in behind it. But not here, this was Rockies limestone. The Trolls were quiet. It seemed they sensed the seriousness of the pitch and had folded their arms over their chests to wait and see how I was going to get up this one. I, too, grew quiet, but it was more an inner calming and narrowing of focus. I had a bolt kit. I knew I could drill if I had to.

I made the first move off the belay. I was never much when it came to grace, but I strove to move like a big sticky blob; slowly and surely across the rock. There was no way I wanted to slip off. I made a few more moves and found a small seam in the back edge of a bump. I managed to slide a knife blade in most of the way. It wasn't excellent, but I knew that if I didn't put it in then it definitely wouldn't hold! Another five feet and I was able to tap a small wire into a seam.

The climbing now consisted of several delicate mantles. I've always hated balance moves. I cursed Mother Nature, the cliff and my position. There was a ledge only four feet above me, but the lip was extremely rounded and smooth. Only inches to my right the rock was running with water, and, of course, that's where the only available foot holds were. It was interesting to note just how well Firé rubber held on the wet limestone! I reached a point where the ledge was right at eye level, but I still couldn't climb onto it. Everything was wet, smooth and sloping. I was run out 10 feet and my legs started to shake. I felt like a little kid trying to climb onto the hood of a car; terrified of going for it for fear of getting stuck halfway and having to abort. I swore at myself, forcing myself to relax and concentrate. Finally I found a micro flake that gave me just enough leverage to pull onto the ledge.

Traversing 20 feet along the ledge brought me out on the west shoulder and into the sun. It was late, I'd had a good day and it appeared that I could descend the west ridge quite easily.

The descent consisted of much swearing and voices echoing, "One slip and you're history."

Back on the trail I was again alone, the flames quiescent. The energy absorbed for now. I allowed myself to feel content with the day.

# Solo

One eye peeks out
of my bivy sack.
Clouds in the Bow Valley.
You know what that means:
Time to go down.

You're wanking out!

I am not.

Yes you are.

No. Clouds are building

Barely a wisp

I can feel it.

Is it precipitating?

No. But my intuition …

Yeah yeah yeah

Don't interrupt!

So you are wanking out?

Fuck you!

You're still a wanker.

This is a judgment call.

OK.
That's enough.
We are going to sleep for another hour.

I wake to bright sunlight.
The loudspeaker
in my brain screams
GO! GO! GO!
This is not a union job!

Go for it man!

No Steve, set up a stance
AND DO IT PROPERLY
You know what you always say
"Fuck around, fuck around,
And pretty soon
YOU WON'T BE AROUND."

Yeah Yeah Yeah.
You and your little sayings.
Just climb the fucking thing.
You're wasting time
and as you said,
the weather is moving in.

Shut up both of you.
This looks serious:
Delicate mantles.

That's a good piece.

Better sling it long though.

You'll fall farther.

Even farther if the rope pulls it out.

That never happens.

It does
and rope drag will kill you if you don't.

What about the ledge?
16 inches might matter.

I'm not saying you can fall off here.

Oh …
I've kicked the piece out

If you blow off now
you'll really auger in.

OK. You're 30 feet out.
Be careful here.
Can you reach down and
wiggle that stopper back in?

                                              No way.
                                  He'll blow off for sure.
                            That last move was irreversible.


                    I hate balance moves:
               Sodden, smooth and sloping.
                  I curse mother nature,
                          the cliff
                    and my position.


                                         You suck at delicate climbing.

I hate balance moves:

No. It's just not my strong area
                                              Like I said.

Can you just be quiet,
I need to concentrate.

                                         Surrrre. I'm glad to.
                                         La-la la-la la.

Shut up!
The rock is wet.

                                              The rock is wet.
                                              The rock is wet.
                                              Ha-ha ha-ha ha!


                    I'm a five year-old
                  trying to pull myself
                 onto the hood of a car,
                 terrified of going for it
              and getting stuck halfway
                 stranded on my belly.
                   Having to abort.
                 Aborting would be bad


                                         You're going to fa-all
                                         You're going to fa-all

I am not.
I'm in control
Please just shut up


                                                                    23

                                   Your feet are slipping.
                                     Your chalk is paste.
                                 Ha! Now you're Elvising!

Relax! Relax!
Drop the heels.
Breathe! Breathe!

                          A micro flake
                       running with water
                      makes more cement
                          of my chalk,
                    but gives me the nudge
                         I need to ooze
                        onto the ledge.


                              Oh I can't believe you made that.
                                     You should go to Vegas.

Good work.
You stayed focused

# The Obsession

"Hi ya Bill, Steve here. I was through Canmore today. There's this line on the north face of Chinaman's just a winkin' — calling out to be climbed. It runs up this parallel slot in the middle third of the face ... "

That was the message I left on Bill Betts' answering machine. We had climbed together twice before, both high energy, high output days. Bill's ever-present drive and enthusiasm I held in the greatest esteem. Moreover, Bill had taught me that it is possible to have fun on climbs while still pushing your own personal limits. Laughter and song often echoed from the crags when we climbed. I had always taken my climbing so seriously, even to the point of repressing mirth and laughter. A friend's dad once exclaimed, "Climbing! Climbing! Climbing! Always climbing! Why don't you go out and have fun once in a while!"

We stopped on the road and looked up to the face. It was 460 metres high. The bottom third would go. The middle third would be steep, but would also go. The next 90 metres or so looked blank. We both went a bit quiet when we saw this section. I blew it off, "a bit of route finding there, eh Bill?" I have always tried not to prejudge a climb. The only way to find out if a route will go is to rub your nose in it.

The first 60 metres went relatively well. There was a noticeable lack of protection, but mainly on moderate terrain. We reached the one-third mark at the bottom of a parallel groove we later nicknamed it "The Gauntlet." The right-hand side of the slot formed a very impressive 90-metre corner.

About 30 metres up, the corner took a jog to the left. With tension from the rope, I leaned out to the left, my feet smeared on tiny rugosities in the rock. I slowly pulled myself to the left on some small flakes. I hung there, half from my harness and half from my purchase on the rock. The tension from the rope was what made progress to the left possible, but it was also doing its best to pull me off the rock. My feet began to slip. I was getting pumped. Son of a bitch! My feet slipped off and I slammed back into the corner. I tried twice more with similar results. Time for the etriers. With my feet again smeared on the rock, my body hyper-extended in an horizontal position and my harness digging into my back, I reached out as far left as possible. I was barely able to slide a knife blade piton upside down into an expanding flake and tap it into place. With the tension from the rope from the right I was able to put my weight on the pin and reach a few metres higher.

A few more intricate engineering-like placements were required before I was again able to climb more easily. But that is part of the beauty of limestone climbing. Nothing is obvious, everything must be thought out; a mental problem with a physical solution. You may not always get the best and quickest solution the first time, or even on the second!

We were now 50 metres up the corner and it was getting late. That last pitch had used up precious hours. It was 6:30 p.m. and we were only halfway up the face. We talked about pushing on and bivying without gear. I had done that before on this face and knew we wouldn't feel a lot like climbing in the morning. Our necks craned to see above. All we could see was a belt of overhangs. It didn't look promising. In addition, I'd been out very late partying the night (or morning) before and had been quietly struggling to keep up with Bill all day. The thought of another night with little or no sleep wasn't very appealing. We descended.

My next attempt, this time with Calgary climber Sean Dougherty, ended atop the second pitch. The air temperature was cool and my mind was elsewhere. I had no job to return to on Monday. I have always needed things to be on a relatively even keel before I can go out and push myself on a serious climb. That day, I just couldn't give it the required level of concentration and commitment. We went home.

Bill and I psyched up for another attempt. This time we were determined to succeed. I went to bed at 9:00 p.m. the night before, and we left Calgary three hours earlier than we had on our first attempt. The weather was crystal clear. But when we reached Canmore our hearts took a dive. We could see the face was running with water! SOB!!

I have always said that climbing a new route can be so frustrating. First you need a route and a desire to climb it. Then you need a partner. Then the weather has to be good and the climb has to be in condition. You must then have the physical ability and the mental preparation to climb it. If any one of these ingredients is missing, you likely won't get up the route.

Bill and I were keen so we decided to rub our noses against it anyway. The first 90 metres of the route was running with water. To avoid this, we completed two new pitches on dry rock to the left of the water. Bill approached me from below, then traversed a little farther to the left, hung his derriere off the ledge and did his business — obviously scared! It was then his turn to take the lead. Again it was wet above so he was forced to traverse to the left. About five metres out, he looked back with a petrified look on his face and shouted, "Watch the rope there Steve!"

I, until then quite relaxed on the belay, jerked upright and locked off the rope.

Bill continued: "If I fall now, I'll really be in shit!" and then laughed in the way that only Bill Betts can. In fact, if he wasn't holding onto the cliff, he would have slapped his knee. Considering his lighthearted attitude, the lead turned out to be a very bold one: Bill was forced to climb a five-metre overhanging wall with a severe lack of protection. I was so scared seconding the pitch I had to call for a tight rope so I wouldn't fall off.

The fourth pitch, too, was running with water. There was no way around it this time. Thankfully, it was Bill's lead and he climbed up the steep corner with water running down his arms. Back at the high point, he shouted, "All right! 5:30! We got here an hour earlier!"

"But Bill, we started three hours earlier ... "

Bill climbed the next 12 metres up the corner to an overhang. There were loose blocks and suspect flakes of rock in the crack. Hanging from the flakes directly above me, Bill looked down with a big smile and said, "Steve, I think this is your kind of climbing up here!" I still don't know how I got the reputation for liking loose rock!

I managed to fight my way through the overhang and pushed on up another 12 metres. The rock was better, but the crack narrowed to a seam. I tried to free it. It was hard and I was tired. I faced an 8 metre fall if I blew it. I hammered in a piton and tried to put some weight on it. Easing down onto it, I watched bug-eyed as it began to pull out. I couldn't get anything else in and it was beginning to get dark. Down we went, having got only 25 metres higher than last time.

The next attempt was with Sean again. Due to the seriousness of the first 180 metres of the climb, we realized it would be difficult to save time on it. We decided to push to the top of the parallel groove and fix ropes back down to the ground, then come back the following day to finish the climb.

On our first day we finally broke out of The Gauntlet. I was excited; I hadn't realized how intimidated I had been by that corner. We'd spent the better part of 12 hours over the last attempts trying to fight our way up it. The face now opened up. The exposure was incredible, further fuelling my desire to climb.

The next day we were back at the high point by 9:00 a.m., ready to rock 'n roll. A beautiful day too! The sun caught the face in the morning so we were able to climb in shorts. We now faced the section of rock that had silenced Bill and I when we had scoped the face out from the road.

As expected the next pitch was intense, a balancing act on loose flakes. For protection in the first 15 metres I had a string of thin pitons hammered in behind some less than solid flakes. I could see that in the next six metres I was going to be much closer to the edge. I didn't have a lot of confidence that those pitons would hold me if I fell. Time to drill a bolt. The wall here was at a low enough angle that I could stand in balance, pull out the driver and begin drilling. My calves began to burn as my boots slowly crept down the sloping footholds. I had to stop every two or three minutes to shake out my aching legs. The sun felt hot and I was sweating. Is it never the perfect temperature up here? Finally the bolt was drilled.

Now I had to pull through a savagely steep slot. The climbing was strenuous and I was breathing heavily. I reached a small stance: "OK gear — I need some protection." I was five metres above my last piece. There were no cracks. The rock was pushing me out. I couldn't stand in balance to drill a bolt. I couldn't put a hook down on an edge of rock because the rock was much too friable. I forced myself to relax; take deep breaths. I carefully scanned the rock and there it was, a little hole less than a centimetre in diameter with a small patch of green telltale moss in it. Aha! I carefully took a small angle piton and drove it in up to the hilt. Oooeee son! The small joys of a climber.

We were now situated two-thirds of the way up the face at a horizontal break. Below us the face dropped away for 300 metres. The sun was gone and we were in the shade. I still had my shorts on. Time for my one-piece pile suit. But of course in order to get into it, I'd have to take my harness off. We were in a hanging stance. I had one foothold and Sean had one. Hmmm ... I ended up having to tie in directly with the rope around my waist while I completed some acrobatics the Mendula Brothers would have been proud of.

I was soon off again and in it up to my neck. I looked down and to the right. My last piece was 12 metres away, a bolt, drilled yet again from sloping footholds. If I fell here and the bolt held, I'd take a 25-metre screamer. I got two nuts behind a flake of rock, and tied them off in equal tension. The climbing wasn't technically radical, but for me it was serious. You had to climb as if on eggshells, continually testing hand and footholds. With such runouts on dubious rock, you can't afford a fall. Your eyes are always searching for that potential crack, hole or seam for a piece of protection. Nothing can be rushed.

This is the kind of climbing that I find the most satisfying. When close to your limit on new and unknown ground, the senses are much sharper. The body and mind function almost like a machine. You must be able to read the rock, be able to decide if what lies above is within your personal physical and mental limits. An error in judgment on this sort of terrain can have grave consequences. Being able to look back 12 metres to my last piece, throw some loose rock off, place a piton and continue climbing is for me what climbing is all about.

The next 25 metres were draining. It was the third three-hour lead of the day on intense ground and I was blitzed. Three metres above was a set of overhangs. Above that was only 90 metres of relatively moderate ground to the top. I stared at the overhangs and I knew I couldn't climb them that day. My body and mind were rebelling. I wanted the route so badly I could almost taste it, yet I couldn't climb a metre higher. Tears rolled down my face as I yelled to Sean that I was coming down. I wasn't all there. My mind kept floating back to my personal problems. And now, failing yet again on this climb, I felt an extreme sense of loss and failure. I had pushed, given 100 percent, my very best and I couldn't do it.

I've always struggled with inner conflicts. On climbs I've sometimes been amazed at the manner in which I can deal with a potentially serious situation. It was black or it was white. If I blew it on a lead, I fell, to try again and again if necessary. Other aspects of life rarely seem so straightforward. Not everything in life can be taken on in the same way as a mountain can.

This turned out to be the last serious attempt on the face that year. Jeff Marshall and I had another go about two weeks later, but it started to rain even before we reached the top of the second pitch. We sat 90 metres up for about half an hour and chatted idly about life in general. It was then that I decided to move out to Calgary permanently to be closer to the mountains.

Nineteen eighty-seven rolled around and the obsession still burned within me. I decided I would first of all break what seemed to be the "North Face Curse." I climbed two other established routes on the face before venturing back onto the wall with Jeff Marshall.

Jeff and I were both pretty fit and climbed the first six pitches through The Gauntlet in record time. Jeff cranked out the seventh pitch beautifully. There we were, two-thirds of the way up at the horizontal break. From the previous year I knew that the overhangs at the top of the ninth pitch would have to be aided. I stretched out and looked left along the break. It appeared that the wall kicked back slightly about 60 metres to the left. The decision was made. I continued along the break for a full 50 metres. The climbing was unbelievable: Straight out left on incut edges, good protection and fantastic exposure. Jeff soon arrived, carried on to the left and climbed a 30 metre corner. Upon seconding the pitch I recognized the spot. The Chris Perry route came up 12 metres to the left. Yeah! I knew it was only two moderate pitches to the top.

Pulling over the top into the sunlight didn't seem real. After all the time and toil it was over. We were pleased and shook hands and howled, but there was no euphoria, no overwhelming sense of accomplishment. We had scored, but the game was by no means over. Inside I yearned for more new and unclimbed rock. I wanted to test myself again and find my true upper limit. This had been a 460 metre climb, my longest new route yet. Could I handle more? I didn't know, but I wanted to find out. Would I ever be satisfied? Again I didn't know. What is it they say, "The two greatest tragedies in a man's life are one, if he doesn't achieve his goals, and two, if he does!" Before our boots were off we were already talking about what was next!

Dave Cheesmond, Ian Bolt, Dan Guthrie, all climbers, and Donald Monro, a school friend of mine, were killed in the spring of 1987 while pursuing their own obsessions. We named the route "Remembrance Wall" in their honor. And in their honor I hope we may all continue to pursue our own dreams and desires. And with these burning passions keep a candle lit for them.

# Jimmy and the Kid

Back at my high point, I felt again the first in a series of small sharp holds. The limestone cut into the fleshy pads on my fingers. I was aware of the sun on my neck, the rack sling on my shoulder, my presence on the cliff. Too aware, but not of the rock around me; rather of my presence in another place removed from the cliff; somehow above and away as though I was watching myself pound in a piton and dip into my chalk bag. Observing almost as one might observe a gladiator from the rows of stone in Coliseum walls, sitting quietly in the heat, watching his struggle for survival within the arena. I was preoccupied with the clatter of chariots on cobbles in the streets behind rather than with the clash of iron on iron below, but still aware that my reality lay in the arena, down there in the dust and not here at this vista, nor in the clamor from the streets behind where horses' hooves clicked on the hard stone ...

The hard stone ... My eyes focused again on my white knuckles wrapped firmly around the shaft of my hammer. Almost shocked, I heard only the echo of its last blow. In this state I knew the arena would show no mercy. I had grown to recognize this feeling and had learned to act on it. Unlike the gladiator, I had a choice.

Could this be true enthusiasm: Failing without frustration? Pumped already, I was still 15 feet below the crux moves. Uncharacteristically, the idea of backing off the pitch did not disappoint me.

On every move, on every pitch, I strive to measure the difficulty and danger of the climbing against my mental and physical capability as well as my ability to focus on the task at hand. I continuously make the decision, "to climb, or not to climb." Here I concluded "not to climb."

By no means was I shocked. I knew I wasn't fit. The idea had been to go out with the Kid and have a good time.

In an earlier time I'd have been flushed with frustration. Partners were relevant only in that they made a more difficult route possible. Today I was having a good time just being out with the Kid, even though I was about to lower off, defeated by a difficult section.

I rapped back down to the belay. "Sorry, old man. I'm just not tough enough for it right now; must have had the devil up my ass when I led it the last time."

In four years I had not backed off a limestone lead. I had been proud of the fact, perhaps even quietly arrogant. But now I was content to let the Kid take over. Both of us knew it was OK to climb hard, scary pitches; but we had learned that they had to be done safely and in control. There was no anger or frustration in the fact that I was now unable to climb a pitch I had led just over a year ago.

Bringing tension onto the belay slings, I strained above to see if Jeff had reached the high point and hollered, "Don't be shy to drill a bolt up there if you have to."

The pitch had been led without it, so technically it would be unethical to drill one. But we were here to climb and have fun, not break a femur.

In these last years we had learned the fragility of our egg-like bodies and the Kid did not hesitate. He put a bolt in.

Rather than second the pitch, I clipped on the jumars and lowered out of the belay in a complex system of tension, leaving a minimum of gear behind. A favorite motto of mine in my formative years had been, "I make up with enthusiasm what I lack in experience." It seemed now that I made up with experience what I lacked in fitness!

Enthusiasm? I believed it was still there, but in a different form from what it once was. Then I'd had what I still consider to be one of the best day's climbing of my life on this cliff. I had been on fire, a rebel with a desire to climb at the cutting edge of my ability, to howl in the face of protectionless pitches, to roar on new terrain. Then I was lean, real lean. A set of 60 pull-ups was no problem. The healthy dissatisfaction that I lived with daily had spurred me on to do bigger, better and increasingly more improbable projects.

"Wild boys always get their way!" we said.

Since then we had learned there are things we have no power or control over; things you can't change no matter how fit, strong or lean you are.

When a fellow climber falls, reality overwhelms the power and joy in the struggle of difficult climbing. Naive, passionate enthusiasm becomes pain; fervor, folly; valor, vainness. All become futile.

Shrouded in cloud, we cried out into the mist. On the north face of Lougheed, Brian Wallace had fallen. Gone, hopefully, to another place where he could continue to be the wild boy he truly was, getting his way.

32

The rain first appeared sympathetic, comforting almost, to our mourning spirits. Even the first chill in our damp bodies seemed to help deaden the guilt of our own survival, though soon it would threaten it.

With vengeance we pounded piton after piton into the rain-drenched rock, questing continuously for the crack or seam into which we could bury our iron. There were no thoughts of our friend or his death. Only of the task: To get away from this place, this storm, this north face, an arena turned savage.

The wall went dark earlier than it should have. Mist clung to us and to the dripping limestone. Soaked wet through, our fevered minds heavy with the day's events, we cleared rubble from a small ledge to form our perch for the night. Snow collected in our collars, chilling our already chilled bodies.

At first it seemed right, honorable almost, to endure this for our friend, with our friend. We were alone, but not so alone; cold, but not so cold. Brian was with us, pushing us.

"No one sleeps tonight."

Jeff's voice cut the silence. I made no reply. He didn't expect one. Both of us continued in our preparations for the night.

To make room for my numb feet I pulled my rock shoes and chalk bag out of my pack. I knew I probably wouldn't be able to find them in the morning. I didn't care.

Somehow, in the gloom Jeff could see the top pocket of my pack folded over onto my lap. "James, can you get that other chocolate bar out?"

I heard the question but didn't comprehend it. Drifting away, I soon believed he had not said anything. Vaguely I became aware of half a chocolate bar being stuffed into my mouth.

Why weren't "they" coming with hot chocolate or blankets I wondered? Gazing into the snow-filled blackness: "There's that cliff below us and that shale slope. They'll never get up them ... in the dark ... in the snow ... "

I stood up on the ledge. More snow fell into my collar. My body rattled harder. "Jeffrey, you're going to have to take care of me."

There was no reply; I didn't expect one. We both knew that in the next 800 feet of steep, snow-covered shale there would be no anchors. Together we would be alone like gladiators at the mercy of the arena. We had no choice.

That was almost a year ago on the steep, rotten north face of Lougheed just across the valley. The enthusiasm we shared now was far different from that of our naïve howls of '86 and '87. Somehow I felt old.

On the last pitch my limbs felt heavy and I moved slowly. Topping out, I looked left toward the summit, thinking that there I might find an answer. Wind lifted the hair under my helmet. I crouched and pounded in a belay station. Looking back down the route, I tried to muster a howl, but it was flat and empty. I didn't try again. Why had I come? There was no answer. I didn't expect one.

# The Wildboys

The healthy dissatisfaction
that I lived with daily
spurred me on
to bigger, better
and increasingly more improbable projects.
Sets of sixty pull-ups were no problem.
Wildboys always get their way we said.
We howled in the face
of protectionless pitches.
Roared on new terrain.
Cut the edge of our abilities.

And then we learned:
When a fellow climber falls,
reality overwhelms the power
and the joy in the struggle
of difficult climbing.
Naive passionate enthusiasm
becomes pain;
fervor, folly;
valor, vainness.
All become futile.

The rain at first
appeared sympathetic,
comforting almost
to our mourning spirits.
The first chill in our damp bodies
seemed to help deaden
the guilt of our own survival.

Piton after piton we pounded
into the rain-drenched rock,
questing continuously for a crack or seam
into which we could bury our iron.

There were no thoughts
of our friend
or his death.
Only the task
to get away.
Away from this place.
This storm.
This north face.
An arena turned savage.

Snow collected in our collars
chilling already chilled bodies.
It seemed right,
honorable almost,
to endure this
for our friend.
With our friend.
We were alone.
But not so alone.
We were cold.
But not so cold.

Why aren't they coming
with hot chocolate and blankets?
Gazing into the snow-filled blackness:
There is that cliff below us
and the shale slope.
They'll never get up them
in the dark.
In the snow.

Brian has fallen.
Gone, hopefully,
to a better place
where he can continue to be
the Wildboy he truly was.
Getting his way.

# The Gladiator

I feel again
the first in a series
of small holds.

I am aware
of the sun on my neck.
The rack sling
on my shoulder.
Too aware …
But not of the rock.

Rather of another place
removed from the cliff.

It's scary
'cause I'm watching myself
pound in a piton and
dip into my chalk bag.
I'm screaming that
I must pay attention.

But I am a spectator
sitting in the heat.
Breathing the dust.
Watching myself
— a gladiator —
from the rows of stone
in the Coliseum walls.

CLIP THE GOD DAMN PITON!
GRAB THE FUCKING SLING!
I do not hear myself.

The gates are open.
Lions enter my domain.
There is a clatter of
chariots on cobbles
that further distracts me.
Horses hooves click
On the hard stone.
But I am alone
— a  gladiator —
at the mercy
of the arena.

# Quantum Leap

I stood there in the fading light, on the ledge, the pack on, my belay clean save for one wire, my jumars already on the not yet fixed rope. I held the cams open with my thumbs and waited. I knew from experience that the rope would jerk up a few feet and then I'd hear the snapping of a carabiner gate as the rope was fixed. I stood there, feeling like Ben Johnson at the starting gates. We were close to the top. An 80 foot pitch after this — max. The sun was already down. A half hour of twilight remained, maybe ...

The jerking rope, a distinctive click, and the gun went off in my head. I sprinted up the rope. Flicking most of Jeff's gear out with the rope before I even got to it. A bolt. Fuck the hangar. Fuck a controlled pendulum. I ran sideways along the rock to make the rope straight and blasted up the last 20 metres to the station.

No time for a "nice lead James," rather a "James! Five quick draws, bolt kit, hooks and wires. That's it!" Jeff clipped gear to me while I put on my rock shoes. In two minutes I was off on the lead padding my way up the steepening ramp to where it became vertical. I was 30 feet off the belay with no gear in. I had one large flat hold to work with. Above, the wall steepened even more and was too featureless for me to feel confident to launch onto it given the progressively blackening sky.

I placed a hook on the flat hold and tapped it lightly with my hammer. With both hands as my belay, I bounced lightly on the hook. It held. But I was not happy. If it blew I would take a 60 foot factor two, hit the ramp below and break both my ankles. And that was the best case.

I scanned the rock and found a small indentation the diameter of a pencil. Quickly I positioned a second hook on this nubbin and adjusted the sling so that both hooks were in equal tension. Again with my hand-hold belay I aggressively tested both hooks. They held.

I gingerly placed all my weight on them. The rock just above was hollow which forced me to drill in the more solid rock off to the left. But at the same time I had to keep my lower body and legs absolutely still so as not to disturb the hooks. For the next half hour

I contorted my torso and drilled. My legs cramped and then went numb. It was dark now. Jeff asked every 10 minutes how it was going. The second time, in a rare instance given the always cordial nature of our interaction, I snapped back, "James, I'll let you know when it's handled." I was gripped, tired and focused.

Finally I clipped the bolt. Rope in and I was off into the blackness. Three tricky moves and my fingers sunk into a hidden rail. I traversed the rail right to a ledge. A short chimney led out to the top where I sat while Jeff jumared the pitch.

Coiling the ropes, I said aloud, "Fuck!"

Jeff said, What?"

I said, "Fuck! This is a serious game."

A week later in retrospection I concluded, "If that's what it takes to turn me on, I'm going to die. If I have to push the limits of my physical and mental ability, on new ground, with self-inflicted time constraints, in the dark, at the technological limit of my equipment in order to get excited any more — sooner or later I am going to fuck up."

It was no longer enough to merely nudge the constraints. I had to demonstrate my mastery of critically wounding or fatal situations. A sneeze, a small mistake, a bird, a pebble or an insect at these moments could mean the end of life as I knew it. Or merely the end.

Quantum Leap was my last serious climb.

# Retirement, Reflection, Rebirth
## 1991-1996

These years saw a reflection on the nature of risk and a pragmatic development of risk management principles.

I also had flashes where I felt compelled to re-experience, if only for a few hours or a day, the heightened awareness that comes from radical exploits.

# The Psycho/Physical Edge

A letter from my brother:

*Stephen,*

*Since I heard the news, I have been feeling really bad. It hurts when someone's dreams are gone forever. I sense your sadness. I know your frustration: Dad told me you did everything you could, hanging from the ropes on that vertical wall, in order to revive your friend. There is pain when a spirit is lost.*

*Brother, I understand the danger of climbing, and it will always be there. When a fellow climber dies, it is like someone took the song out of the birds ... and all that is left is the birds. Try to comfort your friend's family if you can.*

*Dad told me the story of the accident. That north face of Lougheed must be a savage place. Dad said you could have got the chop just trying to retreat from the wall. Man, I didn't want to go to work today. "Throw away the shovel and run!" You know, Mom says that when you are climbing she pretends as though you are in the Vietnam war ...*

I could envision our mother, alone in our family room late at night, gazing up at my picture on the wall. She would be dealing with her fears of my climbing in the same way she had seen her parents deal with the tragedy of friends and a nephew sent off to war. But she never told me not to go climbing. Rather, she would put an emergency space blanket in each of my climbing jackets, along with a lighter and extra batteries for the miniature flashlight she had bought for me and cleverly slung on a shoelace. "See," she said as she demonstrated the principle, "you can hold it in your teeth and keep your hands free to climb!" That little light has saved me from more than one cold bivouac.

Excited, she would burst into my room, "Look at these gloves! Jeff Lowe uses them for mixed climbing." One morning I woke to pack my climbing gear (which was spread out all over the living room of my parents home) to find my system of tarps and green garbage bags replaced by a Gore-Tex bivy sack with a note attached:

"Pay me later. Don't tell your Father."

Those were early days, naïve days. The summer of 1988 had been different. A friend and climbing partner had been killed during our attempt on the unclimbed north face of Mount Lougheed in the front ranges of the Canadian Rockies. My parents, I knew, were shaken.

Over Christmas dinner that year, I was surrounded by a table of questioning and sullen eyes. I knew the worth of my passion for the mountains was in doubt, and the payback of the risks taken was in question. I tried to explain both the different kids of danger present in the mountains and my actions to combat those dangers. Over the years I had developed a climbing philosophy, a philosophy of survival that embodied what I call "The Psycho/Physical Edge."

Objective danger, I explained, is that over which you have no control. It exists to the same degree for every climber at any instant of time, whether with 10 years or 10 weeks of climbing experience. Things like avalanches, loose rocks and weather conditions are objective dangers. Each climber does his best to avoid them. However, if these dangers occur during a climb they are accepted as a given.

The other form of danger is subjective danger. Subjective factors are those elements of risk which fall within a climber's locus of control. These factors include a climber's level of experience, physical and mental endurance, gymnastic ability, the ability to focus, concentrate, relax and solve problems under stress, and a climber's technical knowledge of systems and rope work.

The Psycho/Physical Edge exists as a measure in all of us, determining what level of seriousness and/or difficulty a climber is physically and mentally capable of dealing with. This measure is not cut and dried. For example, a climber could physically be capable of completing a given set of moves, but without the safety of a rope or protection the sequence might be psychologically overwhelming. The situation may also occur where the climber is mentally capable, but physically unable to complete a given sequence. Accurate knowledge of one's physical and mental capabilities is crucial for safe climbing.

No one can climb at the true upper limit of his or her's ability all the time. What may be well within your range on one day might be foolish for you to attempt on another. Your limit may exceed your partner's on a given day, while his may exceed yours the next day. Be aware that your Psycho/Physical Edge may change its position in a matter of hours, or even minutes, depending on the nature of your current situation or your state of mind.

State of mind is a critical factor affecting climbing ability. Your mental endurance, ability to concentrate for long periods of time and your ability to relax and focus under stress, determine your climbing potential. Ask yourself: What has been happening in my personal life? Am I distracted or stressed more that usual? Am I exhibiting excessively negative or positive thought patterns concerning the situation on hand?

Physical capabilities are easier to define and measure. They include physical endurance, gymnastic ability and general health. Consider: Have I been sick lately. Am I sleeping and eating properly? How much climbing/training have I been doing? Can I exert myself hour after hour, day after day, and still remain in control?

Many of these life factors seem to have little to do with the act of climbing. However, they constitute the core of The Psycho/Physical Edge. An assessment of these factors, along with the implementation of your acquired climbing judgment, will enable you to evaluate a situation correctly.

Judgment comes from experience. Experience is not "what happens to you," but rather your ability to apply found knowledge to other more complex situations. Proficiency and effectiveness must be worked on during each climb. It is essential to learn the many ways to solve the same problem. Your rope work and climbing systems must become second nature. Many suggest that if you survive enough experiences, and learn from them, you will acquire good judgment.

The philosophy of The Psycho/Physical Edge is the climber's tool. This tool supplies the climber with a process with which he or she can evaluate alternatives and make decisions regarding a particular ascent.

Apart from objective danger, the greatest risk for an experienced climber occurs at the instant he steps beyond his Psycho/Physical Edge. While climbing you must evaluate your own physical and mental capabilities and then accurately balance them against the difficulties and dangers of your position. This analysis must determine if, indeed, you are capable of dealing with the given situation. This process must continue for the duration of the climb and you must act on this analysis, even if it sometimes involves retreat.

By monitoring and staying within your physical and mental limits you can reduce the risks to those that are purely objective. The instant a climber steps beyond his Psycho/Physical Edge he has, by choice, stepped into a region of unnecessary danger. It is unfortunate, but many deaths occur this way. Know yourself. When facing a serious climb or lead you must cut through everything you think you are and know exactly what you are. You must decide if "what you are" is capable of dealing with the given situation. The crux of any climb is to determine the true edge.

If you choose to climb into a situation beyond your capability, you often make that discovery only when it is too late to change your mind. You have blown it. The situation rapidly goes out of control. You have climbed yourself into a cul-de-sac where there are no options. You fall, sustain an injury or are killed. It is important to recognize that outside the realm of objective danger it is your own fault if you die.

During the first ascent of "The Gambler" (5.11), a climb on the north-facing Rimwall, the rain had just stopped. Thunder boomed and cloud still surrounded us. I used a sock coated in chalk to dry my hand and footholds. Three hundred feet of hard climbing separated us from the top of the wall, it was late and there was no time to wait for the rock to dry. I wiped and dried my way up the steep wall to a point just below a bulge in the rock 25 feet above the belay. I hung there, poised precariously on the damp holds. With the precision of a goldsmith I used the pick on my rock hammer in an attempt to tap a wire into a bottoming crack. At the same moment my partner Jim voiced his opinion, "Your idea of a gully is ludicrous!" His voice lashed out at me.

Stung by his words and struggling to speak calmly, I hissed, "Look, I can't climb this alone. I need your help! I can't do it by myself!" The terrain was serious. I knew I could not deal with it mentally without support from the lads. From Choc, who was also below, came "Give 'er nails, man!"

Jim remained silent and I continued.

Fifty feet later, out of balance and breathing heavily, I blinked and snorted to clear chalk dust from my eyes and nostrils. Leaning back on my finger tips, I could see that the rock above me continued to overhang slightly. Consciously I placed my fingers more securely on a square-cut finger hold and adjusted my left toe to take some weight off my arms. Making a quick glance down 30 feet to my last piece, I saw that if I fell from here I would hit a ledge before the rope came tight. Falling off in this place was not an option. It is in a position such as this that The Psycho/Physical Edge must be applied most accurately.

My arms began to tire. Searching for an opening in the rock, my eyes scanned the length of a micro seam only inches away. Could I pound a knife blade piton into that seam? The protection would be appreciated to say the least. But to try and fail to get a piton in would waste valuable strength. Stopping to drill a bolt would waste valuable time and mean a certain bivouac in uncertain weather. Could I focus enough to climb the next 20 feet without any protection? I felt good. I felt strong. There appeared to be a line of holds. Analyzing, I hung there …

The analysis was based on an evaluation of my mental and physical state; knowledge of my ability balanced against what I judged the difficulty and danger to be. I assessed, then began to climb.

As I climbed, the evaluation continued. Good hold? Yes. Place foot. OK. Uh, no. Further left? Yes. Good? Yes. No! Loose, can't trust that one. Move after move I judged whether I could complete the sequence without falling. As I progressed upward the decision was continuously remade: To climb or not to climb. It was this process that allowed the completion of this particular pitch, which in retrospect still stands as my most serious and situationally involved lead to date.

Another factor which directly or indirectly affects the position of your Psycho/Physical Edge and the effectiveness of your decision-making is the completion of case studies on problem solving, protection and how well you placed it, choice of climbing partners and intuition. Case studies can help you prevent mishaps and solve problems more efficiently when they arise. Learn the best way to do things and never take short cuts. Your rope work and your systems are your base. Errors in this domain are unacceptable. Slow and sure is better than quick and out of control.

Learn to be an artist at placing protection both when it is hard to find and difficult to place. The seriousness of any given section of rock is directly related to the amount and quality of protection placed. A master can find protection where others cannot and thus can venture safely onto terrain that would be suicidal for others.

When contemplating serious climbs, choose your partners carefully. Good friends don't necessarily make the best climbing partners for a proposed route. This sounds cold blooded. It is.

Intuition shows its power in action, though its force is sometimes diminished by the introduction of the rational. Intuition works best when it is simply trusted. The weather may be good, you may be feeling strong, you may even feel motivated and want the route, but if for some feeling you don't want to go … don't go! The mountain is not going anywhere. As a climber it is essential that you seriously consider whatever conclusion, rational or irrational, that your intuition dictates.

Pushing your Psycho/Physical Edge forward must be done with extreme care. The idea is to push in such a precise manner that you never step beyond it, while still forging ahead into new levels of experience. The moment you overstep your mental and physical capabilities is the moment you lose control. The line is very fine, and every time you step beyond your Psycho/Physical Edge, you unnecessarily increase your likelihood of death or injury. Unfortunately, even with extreme care and psycho/physical evaluation, death and injury will continue to be a part of climbing. Objective hazards and human error are the factors that can never be triumphed over.

If a partner takes a fall or is badly hurt, you may suddenly be in charge. If you have never been in this position it is difficult to know how you will react under such stress. If you have been through a case study of the scenario, you will benefit from it. If you believe you will act well, if you envision yourself acting calmly and with precision, you will. Your body may rebel, but you must make those shaking hands work the ropes. There are no options. Your actions in these moments are critical.

What if your partner stops breathing right there beside you? The two of you just hanging from the ropes. He is lost. You are alone. It would not be a time for sadness or anger. The door in your mind to these emotions must slam shut. You have work to do. It becomes your job to get yourself down while you still have the strength and capability to do so. This must be all that exists. There will be time for grief later. It is essential that you act automatically. Your systems of descent must be second nature. Your survival depends on your mental and physical capacity to deal with the situation.

Even now, four years later, I still pause and think of my parents picturing me in battle, and of the summer that ended my naïve days in the mountains; a summer where a friend's last breath was taken in my arms. If I had gone to Vietnam, perhaps my parents would have sent me a camouflage kit for my helmet, or fingerless gloves, maybe some photographs — and a letter from my brother. What could he say? A friend had been killed.

*... so life goes on and you have to feel all the pain until you become strong again. Never let go of what is important to you. Keep climbing. And Steve, use your judgment. Be careful.*

*Thinking of you always,*
*Gerard*

# The Gambler

The rain has just stopped.
Lightning continues to flash.
Thunder booms all around.
Three hundred feet separate us
from freedom.

It is late.
The wall overhangs above.
No time to wait
for the rock to dry.                    ⟶

One thousand feet up
In a femur-fracturing situation.
It's already 6:00 p.m.
We're miles from home.
It is all very clear:
Falling off in this place
is not an option.                    ⟵

From damp holds I tap in
like a goldsmith
a couple of too small wires
into a bottoming crack.
The eggshell bulge is
awkward and loose.
A sock coated with chalk
becomes my best friend
and helps maintain
my purchase.
I pad my way up

the steep ramp
until below the
overhanging wall.
Fifty feet later,
out of balance
on my fingers,
breathing heavily,
I blink and snort
clearing chalk dust

from my eyes
and nostrils.
The rock above
still overhangs.
Thirty feet below
my only piece
practically a clothes pin
anchors my line.
Like I always say,
If you DON'T put it in
it definitely WON'T hold.

# The Rage

The pot belly of my business law professor hangs over the projector as he wheezes business and legal cynicism. He scratches notes on the plastic sheet that his chubby hand fumbles with. Mon professeur, I think, he waxes on about the Supreme Court setting precedent in the reading and interpretation of the laws. The reinterpretation of the meaning of a word or phrase, it seems, could change the whole colour of a defense or argument, that in turn could affect thousands of people. By no means are most issues black or white. It seems to me that a lot of time, money and effort is spent on analyzing grey.

I am intrigued by the importance and subtleties of semantics, this championing of grey. At the same time, however, I chortle at my intimate knowledge of at least one arena of truth. My mind slips easily out the door of the lecture theatre and into the hall, first prancing and then racing, until soon, as though propelled by a gas-fired jet engine, it smashes through the brick work that makes up the end of the hallway. The hammer in my head pounds as my heart pumps to meet this new demand. My lungs burn as the cool breeze passes my teeth. Away I storm, out and over the prairie grasses west of Calgary and soon, like a space-age fighter pilot, land on the pitching deck that is the gravel road into the parking lot at the base of Yamnuska. In the haze of the rising dust disturbed by my Toyota Tercel, again I chortle. It had been a while — a long while — since I have done battle.

In my youth and all through the years of my limestone apprenticeship, it was never a question of wanting or not wanting to battle. It was a question of having to. The allure was the honesty, the honesty required by self and the challenge of confronting the brutality that was inherent in the game. You had to develop tools to deal with such conditions: Two being experience and fitness, and the other "The Rage" — a valuable tool if you can harness it, deadly if you can not. The Rage allows a climber to tap into his innermost primal energy. Beyond sexual or quest drive, it is the fire that allows for human life and evolution, and provides the driving force for survival.

The Rage is not meant for use in everyday life, just as jet fighters are not meant for negotiating traffic. Periodically I have been caught in my fighter plane stranded in five o'clock downtown traffic attempting to turn right on 4th Avenue towards the mountains. The jet engines are screaming, sweat soaking the back of my shirt, its collar strangling me. The thrust of air from the jets rips dust and paper into a grey cloud, the venturi force tearing manhole covers out of place and hurling them down the street. Down-townees turn and flee from the violence. Finally, I jump from the cockpit, the noise bursting my ear drums. I manhandle the plane's nose around the corner until it points straight west. Then I frantically climb back in, bludgeon the wheel one more time, tear the tight collar away from my neck, popping six or seven buttons onto the cockpit floor, and again endeavor to take off. A frustrated commuter honks his horn. My lips curl into a snarl as I bare my incisors and growl like a werewolf, spraying saliva and mucus onto the wind screen as I fully engage the thrusters.

Dismounting from the cockpit of my vehicle, I begin to garb up for the adventure. A hiker passes by. Glancing at her watch, she asks, "What's the rush? Are you camping there?"

"Camping?" My head turns to face her, my eyes targeting hers like heat-seeking missiles. "No," I sputter as I glance at my own watch — 5:14 p.m. — there is no time to describe my exploit. "No. I'm not camping up there." In any other situation, I'd have liked to stay to chat. I am, however, primed up and ready on the flight deck. It is time to fly. I break my personal record on the approach to the base of my first climb. The climb is not radical by anyone's yardstick; it is, however, a personal voyage and for me is good value. As I top out the last rays of sunlight lick the Front Range peaks.

My rock shoes, like pontoons, splay and glide down the scree on the back side of Yam. Soon I arrive at the base of my second route. It is closer to the centre of the face and constitutes 300 metres of climbing; more climbing, I know, than the remaining light — now reflecting solemnly from the arêtes, chimneys and fissures—will allow for.

I stand there breathing deeply. What did I come here for? I came to engulf myself in The Rage.

An instant later I step upward and away from my pack on the scree trail which contours the base of Yamnuska. I pull the straps of my headlamp over my head, much like the fighter pilot would pull on his flight helmet. Slowly and deliberately I pull the straps taut to ensure a secure yet comfortable fit. Another step and I am on the runway that is the initial scrambling to the base where the real technical difficulties begin. I ignite my engines — my focus, my oxygen intake and The Rage — one at a time. My vision goes tunnel as my hands begin brushing stone.

I joy in these movements; my spine tingling with the prospect of the challenges that lie above me. I have not played in the arena for a while. The chalk on my hands feels comforting, the rough limestone under my fingertips relaxing. At this point, my objective is to nudge the edge of my potential into a new realm, in this case not into one of technical difficulty, but into one of situational commitment.

I know that as the sky turns black the white light of my head lamp and my ability to relax and concentrate will rescue me. If my headlamp or abilities fail, I will be forced to bivouac, but I am prepared to risk this consequence for the benefit of my cause: A chance to tap into The Rage, a chance to do battle and reap the overwhelming and immediate gratification of success and stifle into submission any prospect of failure. It is all so clear. By tapping into The Rage, I can reach deeper into myself than anyone pursuing an urban utopia could ever understand. I can bring out my primal instinct and use it as a tool for ascent and survival.

The freshly chalk-coated callouses on my finger tips squeak as I weight the polished limestone flakes and wedged blocks that make up the crux. A smattering of excess white powder falls from my hand upon its contact with the rock. Instinctively I twist my head downward when I see it coming, only to witness the small white cloud careen in the turbulent air and fall, fleeting and floating, 20 feet down to the narrow scree-covered ledge below.

With my head cocked at this awkward angle, I catch the last light of the sky reflecting from the sheen on my forearm. I ponder only momentarily the implications of this fading glow when a bead of perspiration rolls neatly into my left eye. "Not now!" I grimace, exposing my sharp white teeth and blood-red gums. I blink and squint in a focused effort to clear the eye-reddening sting. My jaw muscles pulse, creating a throbbing vice in my jaw. The force on my teeth, it seems, is great enough to crush easily any of Yamnuska's loose rock into gravel. My good eye darts like an India rubber ball thrown hard in a rapidly-closing cavern. Right handhold — good, left foothold — OK, right foot — move to a new smear, take weight off left arm, move left forearm to left eye socket and brow. "Aah." I finally arrest the flow of tears.

In the process, however, I have skewed my bandana. The chalk on my fingertips turns to paste as I readjust the saturated silk cloth.

"Down time! Down time!" I hiss as I wipe my hands on my shirt and then chalk for the second time in 10 seconds my left hand. My left eye, now clear, steals one more glance at the progressively graying horizon.

"OK. Time to go to battle stations."

My vision again goes tunnel. I reach deeper until soon I am completely engulfed in The Rage. I chuckle at the boost, my jaw relaxed.

This energy, so clean-burning, allows me to stand above all my intellectual and emotional fears, even above the unnecessary concern that I have about the potential physical danger I am in. Not that I am unconcerned, but perhaps my desire for this higher-order mental state through a sequence of intrinsically risky acts is akin to a cocaine addict's lust for a similar frame of mind. They say, "A line makes you feel like a new man. And what does the new man want? — another line!" This, I postulate, reaching for yet another handjam, is not unlike me, except that I wanted another "line" on Yam.

My feet and headlamp skid and dance once again across the snow and scree that constitutes the back side of Yamnuska. The internal thrusters, now quiescent, purr along at idling speed as I taxi back into the gravel parking lot at the base of the mountain.

A fine evening indeed. I chortle at my intimate knowledge of yet another arena of truth. Pulling my bicycle from the car, I mount it as though straddling a missile, switch my headlamp back on, lock in the target (my home in Calgary over 85 kilometres away) and with a shriek of delight fire it. As I speed along the 1A Highway under a star-filled sky I grin in anticipation of the drive I will make with a friend back to Yam to pick up the car later that day. It is 1.30 a.m. In six hours I will pedal easily through the morning traffic.

A week later, a fleshy five o'clock-shadowed jaw waxes further about the payment scheme for work or research done in grey. My vision goes tunnel as it burns two holes in his padded chest. My spirit leaps from my seat in rage and the lecture hall booms with my silence: "Let me tell you about value ... "

# The Rage

Failing my headlamp or ability
I will be forced to bivouac.
I am prepared to risk this consequence
for the benefit of my cause:
A chance to tap into The Rage.
A chance to do battle
and reap the overwhelming gratification
of success. Stifle into submission
any prospect of failure.
My jaw muscles pulse.
CLIMB MAN!
CLIMB LIKE A BEAST!

I hurtle myself up the cliff,
my breathing deep and focused,
my foot-work accurate and precise.
I'm dancing now, so dialed
I feel no pain. So intensed
only my momentum exists.
A sharp rock could take off my hand
and I'd merely grimace and
place the useless flesh in my teeth
and continue to charge my way
up the crag, fully engulfed
in THE RAGE.

I grapple the top-stones, my jaw relaxing
and I growl: MASH GOOD!
I leap over cliff bands,
partly with grace and agility,
partly like a rolling man-hole cover
barrelling through rocks and scree.
I stumble only once, tumble
but roll like a dynamo,
then cartwheel like a gymnast
with hardly a scratch as I howl
OOOOEEEE SON!

# It's Nukin'

Frothing with white water, my kayak lurches as I hurtle over a small waterfall. The raging current bucks my boat like a wild bull at the Calgary Stampede rodeo. Instinctively, I jam my paddle in the water in a last ditch attempt to prevent being tossed into the drink by this large animal. My paddle stabs the water more like a spear and goes deep into the raging trough. Instantly, the paddle is ripped from my hands. In the next moment I am upside down, my helmeted head only feet from large submerged rocks. With my paddle gone, there is no chance of completing an Eskimo roll. Somehow I have broken the cardinal rule of whitewater kayaking: Never let go of your paddle.

Actually, I had not intended to go kayaking in Washington that week. I was on vacation trying to learn how to windsurf in the Columbia River Gorge in Oregon. I had sailed once or twice in Alberta, and then someone mentioned that "The Gorge" was the Yosemite of windsurfing. Like clockwork, winds raged often in excess of 60 miles per hour in the summer. The sun heats up the desert. The hot air over the desert rises and cool air from the coast tears through a gash in the mountain range made by the Colorado River. It is a classic thermal wind. It seemed to me that if I wanted to learn how to windsurf I should go to the capital. So off I went. Alas, by some fluke of nature there were many days in row without any wind whatsoever. It was too hot to go cycling. There was a climbing area five or six hours to the south, but I did not want to take off down there just in case the wind did pick up.

There was, in fact, another reason why I did not want to go rock climbing. In January of '94 I'd rediscovered my passion for extreme climbing for the first time since my retirement in '90. For four months I had trained five days a week and had made attempts on some big unclimbed alpine projects in the Rockies. Two partners and I had come close to bagging a route on the east face of Mount Chephren, but storms and bad avalanches had forced us to retreat on three attempts in as many weeks. And then, by the second week in May the passion had vaporized. With it went the long list of first ascents yet to be done, leaving me in a kind of a daze. The platform I'd been building on had disappeared. I did not understand it. Could not fathom it. Tried for another three weeks to force it, but the flames no longer shot out of my finger tips. No fire. No desire. Training became awkward. Climbing, dangerous. Bouldering, like a trip through Wendy's late night pick up window. With the projects list gone, the goals removed, my training had no direction. I had never climbed for fitness. And when I tried I just got bored and could not take it seriously. So by July I was still in mourning over the death of these aspirations and the loss of the path. I was startled that the oak tree of intensity for climbing could shrink and shrivel itself back into the acorn. And this acorn continued to irritate me like a large stone in my shoe. It was stuck there wherever I went. So that's the other reason why rock climbing was not an option. Windsurfing arrived in my psyche to neatly fill the void.

When the wind doesn't blow in Hood River, the little town is quiet. And hot. People just don't seem to be out, save for a few tourists who saunter along at a cemetery pace. When it's nukin', however, the place becomes electric. "Nukin'" is a term coined by the windsurfing hard core meaning nuclear wind strength. When it's nukin' everyone is in a panic to rig up. People run red lights, double park at the waterfront, talk fast and loud to be heard over the wind. If they do stop at a red light or stop sign beside another sailor, windows are rolled down and it is not uncommon to hear the phrase, "fukitsnukin'!" When it's nukin' people lose common sense, forget to tie their windsurf boards down to the roofs of their cars or even stow their gear properly on the river bank. I have seen a gust of wind pick up a board and sail and hurl it 50 feet across the beach. When it's nukin' windsurfers get rig-stress when trying to assemble their gear and get on the water fast. Even simple tasks become unmanageable; trimming the high-tech fully-battened sails with complicated down-haul and out-haul rigging, impossible. More than one fight breaks out between man and spouse as man charges onto the river to sail, while his rig-stressed spouse can't tie a clove-hitch or struggles to attach her mast foot to her board.

So here I am, taking one of my precious weeks off from my engineering job in Calgary in order to learn how to sail in The Gorge and there is no wind. Surely I can find a surrogate adventure down here somewhere ...

From the "Gorge Guide" I read that there are rafting tours down the White Salmon River just across the border in Washington. Rafting, however, is not for me. No challenge. Rafting is for tourists who want the "feel" of an adventure without having to experience the risk, the decision-making and the hard work of a "real" adventure. It is merely a roller coaster on the water. Might as well go to Disneyland. Kayaking, on the other hand, had always been a closet interest of mine. For a time, I used to say, if I were not a climber, I'd be a kayaker. Indeed, I had peered out of that closet and had had one or two kayaking lessons over the years — had even done an Eskimo roll in a swimming pool once. Hmmm, I think, if they can raft it with garden-variety tourists, surely it must be kayakable, even for a novice like myself.

So I amble on over to the boat rental shop at the marina in Hood River and enquire about kayak rentals. The proprietor behind the counter asks, "Can you do an Eskimo roll?"

"Well, I have done one before. But not for four or five years."

"I won't rent you a boat if you cannot complete an Eskimo roll."

We are situated right on the water in Hood River and I suggest, "How about I go out into the marina and practice. You can watch me from here."

The proprietor gets a faint glint in his eye. His lips curl at the edges. He likes that idea. So do I. It seems prudent for me to get dialed back in to my Eskimo rolls before I venture out into real white water. And it would be kind of a fun preliminary test to have to re-learn the roll under some pressure.

Hoisting the kayak onto my shoulder (the boat weighs 40 pounds, heavier with paddle, full body wet suit, life jacket and spray-skirt), I make my way down to the dock, put on my wet suit and climb in the boat. The spray skirt is a bit of a struggle and I nearly spill into the water just getting it on over the deck lip. It is critical, I recall, that the little loop at the front of the spray deck protrude up and not get caught under the elasticized rim of the spray deck. This little loop is effectively your rip cord when you go upside-down. If the skirt does not release, it is impossible to get out of the kayak and you can drown. I close my eyes and practice pulling it off. Then I put the paddle in my hands and repeat the exercise until I am confident that I can complete this task blindfolded with either hand.

From lessons I'd had at camp when I was a kid, I remember that the first step of an Eskimo roll is to practice the hip movements required to absorb the shock of waves and to maintain balance. With one hand on the dock, I begin this hula motion with the boat. I do this for five minutes or so and then begin what I recall is the second step. I grasp the dock with my left hand and slowly and purposefully angle the boat over to 90 degrees. Then by flicking my hips and using the dock for balance, I right the boat. I spend the next half an hour repeating this exercise and slowly increase the tip angle until I have the boat upside down on the water. Similar to a rock climbing boulder problem, I repeat the move over and over again. I begin to discover the most efficient body position for the sequence. I get to the point where I have only slight pressure on my hand as I execute the roll procedure. When I feel I have it dialed, I do it 20 more times. Then I change sides and use my right hand and repeat all the same steps.

The next crucial step is to add the paddle into the process. Deep in the darkest recesses of my memory I recall from the same lessons that the starting paddle position is a critical factor. I remember the start position, but I have to sit and re-create the motion that exerts the force I need to complete the roll. It is not a straight stroke of the paddle. It is more like a fanning motion where the paddle moves through the water in a large arc, much like the propeller on a helicopter. I have to get out of the kayak and sit on the dock to visualize this sequence. As I move the paddle through the water, my body should rotate upward, changing the presentation of the paddle to the water. The axis of rotation is the length of the boat. In theory, I have to keep paddle force perpendicular to this axis of rotation. It is mind-bending to visualize this going on while I am holding my breath upside down in cold water with no one around as a backup if I make a mistake.

Holding the paddle normally, I place the left end of the paddle across the front of the kayak on the right side. The paddle now lies flat on the water with the blade closest to my left hand, also flat on the water. OK — here goes! I purposefully flip the boat and am hanging upside down from my legs, hips and spray skirt. I stare upward at my paddle close to the surface of the water. I want to make sure I have it flat. I wrench the paddle down through the water. The boat and I rotate. My head comes out of the water, but I do not have enough rotation force and I sink back under. Now the question: Do I have enough air in my lungs to reposition the paddle and make another attempt? I think I do, so I reposition the paddle. Again I make sure that the blade is parallel to the surface of the water. Again I wrench the paddle across my body. This time my head and part of my shoulders come out of the water. I do not, however, have enough speed to continue to the upright position and I descend back into the water.

Now I am out of air. Holding on to the paddle with one hand, I reach for the spray skirt loop. The skirt comes off like it's supposed to and I wriggle and fall out of the kayak into the water. I swim the boat over to the dock and empty the water out.

The next six or seven attempts yield the same result. In the effort that follows, I haul on the paddle with so much force that I come right out of the water with too much speed, and like a paddle wheel continue rotating, only to dunk on the other side. I am excited as this is the first time that I have created that much momentum! I reposition the paddle and execute the move again. This time, though, as I am rotating up and over I slap the water with my paddle on the other side to prevent another flip. I stay upright!

The practice session continues until I can roll at will coming out of the water right side first. Then I repeat the process until I am just as confident on the left side.

The proprietor has seen me execute a few rolls so is now willing to rent me the kayak. Placing a scruffy cowboy hat on his head, he explains that, "Rule number one in kayaking is: Don't let go of your paddle."

The White Salmon River features some enticing white water. Below the road there is one section of class III rapids and the rest is class I and II. Above the road there are many class III and IV rapids, finishing with a class V section at the end that many kayakers portage around. The route is popular with rafting companies as well. It seems to me that I should start on the section below the road as a warm up.

I am at the river within an hour of my practice session. Here I add my cycling helmet to my equipment list. Just below the put-in point I can see there is a class III rapid. I paddle slowly into it, trying to pick my point of entry. Somewhere over my shoulder I hear a loudspeaker: "Welcome to the Calgary Stampede!" Instantly the kayak begins to buck like a wild bull leaving the chute. I struggle with the paddle to stay upright. "The Bull" is first head down, then nose high with both feet in the air. Just as I am losing my balance The Bull hurtles over a small drop. The bow of the kayak digs in and I am hit with a wall of water. And then I am upside down. The four-legged whirlwind continues down the river at a thwarting pace. The water ices my face with such a shock that for a moment I am frozen like a deer in the headlights. My head thrashes in rhythm with The Bull's thrusts only inches from large rocks on the bottom of the river. I have held on to my paddle. From my upside down position

I stare up through the cold clear water at the sun's rays dancing through the rivulets above me. I can see the blurry green of leaves on trees, the blue sky and a big white cloud, but refracted and distorted through the rolling surface. This must be what a fish sees as it looks up through the water at the outside world. Simultaneously I am fascinated and gripped with this perspective. Frantically I try to stay calm, reposition the paddle, double check the blade angle and execute my Eskimo roll. I pop up suddenly. There is a roar from the grandstand as the spectators, including the stampede clowns, are astounded at my sheer luck in staying on this wild animal. The clowns are dressed brightly and have mangy yellow hair topped by scruffy cowboy hats. All of their exposed skin, including their faces, is caked in white makeup. The horn blows.

I did it! My first real roll in the real world. But then a jolt of fear shakes through me. Perhaps it is just the cold water? I convince myself that dumping in the first 200 feet of river is just bad luck and I continue down the river.

As it turns out, the crux of this portion of the river was the first rapid. The remainder of the lower river is quite placid and enjoyable. I am having fun.

The next day I head with confidence to the put-in on the upper river. This time I throw a 40-foot piece of retired climbing rope into the boat. I don't really have any plans for the piece of rope, but somehow, given my all my years of climbing, I always feel more comfortable with a piece of rope at my disposal. As I am climbing into the kayak, I decide to clip one end of the short rope to the back of the boat. My thinking is that if I need to do a wet exit, I could swim to the side of the river with the rope in my hand and then pull the kayak to shore after me. To protect my feet from scrapes on submerged rocks, I am wearing snug-fitting windsurfing booties. They have a black sticky rubber sole for keeping a grip on the surface of windsurfing boards and feature a neoprene upper. I have a topo of the river that I tuck in a pocket that I believe should stay dry under the spray skirt.

Right at the entry point there is a class III rapid featuring a rocky chute spewing water. It is frothing at a high speed and really does look like a bull pen. The Bull pitches and jumps from side to side angrily against the gate as I try to climb in. It snorts and grunts as I fumble with the spray skirt. Somewhere underneath, the stampede clowns squeal with delight as they cinch the bucking rope around The Bull's girth, effectively pinching the 2000-pound monster's bulbous testicles. The Bull hammers hooves into the chute with the staccato of a jackhammer. His big head careens. His horns gouge deep grooves in the walls.

Suddenly the doors of the chute open and The Bull lunges out. I am amazed at the acceleration into the arena. The Bull snarls and snorts again and I am splattered with yellow molten mucous that gums to my wet suit. Uncharacteristically, The Bull leaps onto his side. The water is only a few feet deep and moving very fast. I exchange blows with The Bull and dig my spurs in. My paddle immediately hits rock on the bottom of the chute. As I fight to right the boat, spearing the bottom more like I'm trying the kill this large animal, than trying to perform an Eskimo roll, The Bull yanks me bodily down the chute. Every time my face and shoulders come out of the water and I manage to catch a breath, The Bull changes direction and pitches me around like a rag doll. Abruptly I am up against a small rock wall on my right. I am in trouble.

"Okay Stevie, time to pull the rip cord and wet exit."

Letting go of the paddle with my left hand, my hand flaps wildly in the air for a moment. The clowns glance at each other in surprise. I will qualify for extra points for that hand motion. In a panic I grab the loop on the spray skirt and release it. My right hand is flailing under water with the paddle. It hits the bottom, but only throws me off balance. The kayak fills with water as it continues to lurch and buck on its side. I try to shake it off, but am pinned by the rock wall. I lean back, battling The Bull by battering its fur-covered back with my churning legs. I'm stuck. I can't get off this careening animal! The water is too shallow for a conventional wet exit. I am being dragged half on my side, half upside down. I continue to make vain attempts to take gulps of air, but the situation is out of control and I have real fear.

Suddenly The Bull leaps and the stern quarter catapults out of the water and smacks me in mouth. Bright light flashes in front of my eyes. I writhe and twist in a final frenzy of frantic shifts and shoves, and with a conclusive kick escape The Bull. The water chute spits us out into a shallow pool at the bottom. The eight second horn blows. Thank god I am done! A stampede clown emerges from a battered, internally-padded orange barrel to distract The Bull for a moment. I can taste blood. My face is numb. The clowns swim the boat to the bank while I stuff fingers in my mouth to worriedly check my front teeth. They are intact. Bloody fingers inform me that my lip is cut. I glance back up river: I have come only 100 feet. The clowns, seeing that I don't have life threatening injuries, begin mimicking my rag-doll performance and making exaggerating grimaces to the delight of the crowd in the stands. I merely limp to the shore.

It appears I can walk back along the riverbank to my put-in to escape. Downstream is a canyon with 100 foot-high rock walls on either side. If I carry on I am committed to kayaking the whole river. Attempting to confirm this on the river topo, I find it is gone, ripped out of my pocket by The Bull of the river. It's only 10:30 a.m. "What am I going to do the rest of the day if I quit now?" I briefly consider the prospect of wandering around Hood River in the heat at the tourist's cemetery pace.

The blood flow is starting to ebb. I am pleased that I have not broken either my teeth or rule number 1: Don't let go of your paddle. It occurs to me that perhaps the precursor to rule number 1 might be: Don't solo paddle down a whitewater river that you have never paddled before, particularly if you're really just a rock climber on a windsurfing holiday.

Slowly my composure recovers. I convince myself that if I really take my time, I can pull into eddies and get out of the boat to scope the rapids before I shoot them. Besides, I can always portage around one or two rapids if they look too hairy.

And so I stow the climbing rope back in its place, climb back into the kayak and am away down some pleasant class I and II water. The rapids are more like what I paddled the day before and my confidence again builds. I practice ferrying back and forth and entering and leaving eddies. The Bull is nowhere to be seen. The clowns are curiously quiet, their pasty white faces as blank as the faces of professional poker players. I am sure they are up to something. I try to stay in the side eddies where the water is moving more slowly. This should give me time to respond to any rapid ahead.

Very soon, though, I can hear the roar of whitewater. I choose the spot on the bank to beach the boat, and scope out the rapid. The stampede clowns magically reappear, and with a giggle and a wink to the crowd, give the bow of my boat a nudge. Then more aggressively they pull the bow of my little craft into the faster moving water. In vain I attempt to ferry over to the bank, but two clowns grip the boat on either side and push me headlong into very fast flowing water leading to a large drop-off. It immediately becomes clear that I am committed to running this rapid blind.

The water, frothing white, shoots me into a violent mass where currents are shooting in five different directions. My kayak again morphs into a furious Bull. The clowns face the spectators in the stands. With their cowboy hats crushed in their hands, they make exaggerated grimaces with their white made-up faces, throw their hands in the air, then hold their ears, wincing as if they can't stand to watch what The Bull is going to do to me this time. It bucks hard on a standing wave, then twists, trying to throw me over to the right. I respond with a sharp paddle stroke as I am rotating over, but I stab the water more like a spear and my paddle disappears deeper into the raging trough. The Bull then nosedives over the drop and continues his twisting motion. In an instant, a submerged clown, hiding in his dented orange rodeo barrel takes a hold of my paddle and seizes it from my grasp. I am startled at the force. Somehow I've broken rule number 1 in kayaking. The Bull, sensing my loss of control, pounds his hooves into the dirt and with a jerk, his haunches are impossibly vertical. He simultaneously dives and twirls. Now I am upside down, submerged.

The Bull's head, legs and flank continue to churn the water into an air-filled, creamy-white whip. Like a magician, a clown produces a sturdy mug, dips it into the froth, raises it over his head and asks, "Anyone for cappuccino?" My head is only inches from submerged rocks. With my paddle gone, there is no chance of completing an Eskimo roll. I do not hesitate. I pull the loop and wet-exit. Suddenly I am floating down the river, The Bull trotting ahead of me. My paddle! My paddle! I reach into the boat and grab the rope, then yard The Bull over to some boulders on the bank. The Bull is still angry and fights against my tugging. I'm counting the seconds. With strength that only comes from adrenalin, I reel the rope in, grab the large animal bodily and toss it up on the boulders where it quickly morphs back into a harmless kayak. The stampede clowns raise their eyebrows momentarily, purse their lips in surprise and then vaporize the moment they could actually be of some help. My eyes scan the water like laser beams. I have to find my paddle. I can't let it float by me. I cannot!

After what seems like minutes, the river at last releases my paddle from the frothing chute. It floats toward me and I stare bug-eyed and confused. The aluminum is bent at a 90-degree angle at its middle. It floats and bobs through the water toward me like a "V for Victory" being paraded around the stampede arena.

Wading, then swimming into the river, I grab the bent paddle, swim back to the boulders and climb up to the kayak. I can't believe it. That clown must have guided my paddle into a crevice between boulders when I stabbed at the water in my attempt to stay upright. The momentum of the boat along with my death grip on its shaft had snapped it like a dry sapling. I attempt to straighten it. The deformed shank merely parts in my hands and breaks in two. Okay, so I'm up the river with a broken paddle …

I look around to see what my options are at this juncture. On either side of the river are 100 foot-high vertical cliffs. Portaging is not an option. Hiking the bank with the boat in the water is also not an option. I spy a small tree growing next to the river. It is about the diameter of the paddle. Instantly, a yellow-haired clown emerges from his rodeo barrel. He snaps off the sapling and is quick to demonstrate, with the eager and blameless look of a five year old, just how this stick could be used as a splint. This, I explain to his chagrin, still does not get me around the fact that as a kayaker I am way in over my head. I am learning that kayaking is a serious sport and not to be taken lightly. I have a big fear of the river now.

While puzzling my predicament, I scan the cliffs. The first 80 feet are vertical. The last 20 feet kick back somewhat. The piece of old climbing rope I have brought with me is only just over 40 feet long so it will not be long enough to get me to the top of the cliff before I run out of rope. If it were longer, it would be a straightforward if strenuous task to just haul the boat up hand over hand after me. I look for a weakness in the rock. I can not leave the boat behind. It would be a $1000 bill from the rental shop if I came back without it.

One section of cliff features a tree growing on a very small ledge about halfway up. It is about eight inches in diameter — a large tree to be growing on the side of a cliff. If I can manage to climb up to the tree, wedge myself behind it and then haul the kayak up to my position, I might then be able to wedge the boat between the tree and the rock. All the spruce branches should help to hold the boat in place. From this intermediate ledge I should then have enough rope to climb to the top, or at least onto easy ground.

At once I begin analyzing the features in the rock above and below the tree. It is vertical. However, there are weaknesses. I stare for a moment back down the river. The specifics of the river are unknown to me; the river medium even more so. My paddle is broken. Is it less risky to swim or float down the river holding the boat on its tether? And what about that class V rapid at the end. Would I be successful in getting to shore to ensure a portage around it?

My shoes are neoprene wind surfing booties. They have a sticky rubber sole, but will have no edging ability. I will, though, have excellent feel through the bottom of my feet on the rock.

Pulling the short piece of rope out of the boat, I tie one end to the bow of the kayak. I stow my life jacket in the stern along with the broken paddle. When I haul the boat up by the bow, the gear should sit nicely in the back of the boat. Then I pick up the kayak and lean it up against the base of the cliff with the bow end up. This will help me conserve rope and hopefully allow me to get firmly behind the tree before I start hauling.

Wet suit. Do I take it off for the climb? The spruce tree has some sharp-looking branches. I am soon going to be very intimate with that tree. It will have fewer branches when I am done. It also represents a backup. If I slip or get into trouble while trying to negotiate the moves above the tree, I may be able to grab the tree to arrest my fall, or merely jump off and grab it.

I had done this years before at a bouldering area when I was 15 years old. At the top of a 25 foot-high boulder problem, I could not negotiate the final moves over the top. There was a tree with a trunk about four inches in diameter five or six feet behind me. I hung there, 20 feet up for several minutes, unable to climb up or down. As my strength flagged, I got the mad idea to leap for the tree and sprang from the rock like a cat, completing an 180 degree rotation in mid air as my grappling hooks locked around the tree. And then, like a squid, my legs wrapped quickly around the trunk and I slowly slid down the tree like a pole at a fire hall. I decide to leave the wet suit on.

I tie the other end of the rope around my waist with a bowline. This, in fact, was the way that the early pioneers of climbing tied into a climbing rope before climbing harnesses were invented. I don't know for sure, but I think the knot was borrowed from sailors dating back to the old square-rigged vessels. The bowline around my waist is, indeed, my bow line to my boat. I had learned how to climb from my high school machine shop teacher, Jim Fothergill. He had begun climbing in his native England in the early nineteen sixties. Climbing gear had changed, but Jim was a minimalist and even in the 1990s still climbed with just a rope tied around his waist with a bowline. Subsequently, I had done my first leads with a rope around my waist tied with a bowline. In this case, though, it was merely a convenient way to attach the rope to my body.

I study the first section of the rock for a few minutes and then begin to climb. I feel a sense of comfort sweep over me. This is the arena that I know. This is my comfort zone. The rock feels good on my hands. My body relaxes and I do not feel any more my fat and bloody lip nor the scrapes and bruises from my fight with the bull of the river. The sun is on me. The rock is dry. Mysteriously, flames begin to shoot out of my fingertips. I am shocked at the return of the flames.

"Fire and desire! Yeah! Mash Goooood!"

My mourning spirit erupts in a volcano of joy. I glance down and capture a forlorn and disheartened look from the stampede clowns. They simultaneously hang their heads in defeat as they watch the rope, tied to the snout of the once frightening Bull, snake its way up the cliff tied to my waist. One clown buries his white-painted face in his padded orange rodeo barrel like an ostrich.

I chortle, "Yuh uh uh!"

My windsurfing booties even feel natural on the rock. The moves are fluid and partially gymnastic right off the deck, but I am home. It's like throwing open the front door of my parent's home and having the smell of spaghetti fill my nostrils and my mother, hearing me over her shoulder, declare, "Hi hon, I've made your favorite!"

"Aah. Thank you. Thank you. Thank you!"

As I progress I remain confident that if I climb myself into a cul-de-sac I can down-climb this section if I have to. Jim also taught me that the leader does not fall. "You must be able to down-climb anything you up-climb. Always climb in control." This no-fall approach, even in the late nineteen seventies when I was indoctrinated at the age of 14, was aborted by most climbers. But for me it was a great approach to learning how to climb, and later became my most valuable survival tool when the going got tough and run-out; where falling off was not an option. I was admonished early in my leading days by my peers for backing off routes and refusing to hang-dog or demonstrate a willingness to take leader falls. Much later, though, after I had developed some judgment, I was chastised for either taking or risking huge falls. Indeed, there were many that thought I was a psycho. Me? Well, I'm the safest guy I know.

Soon I am 30 feet up and gunning for the tree. I must be well above the river's typical flood line. The rock quality deteriorates slightly and I encounter the first loose rock on the pitch. With Jim I went to the less travelled parts of the Niagara Escarpment in Southern Ontario where the routes were climbed less frequently. Here Jim gave me my first instruction on how to climb loose rock: "Climb as if climbing on egg shells." He instructed a look, listen and feel approach. First study the rock for fractures, tap the hold with the palm of your hand or the toe of your boot and listen for a hollow sound associated with a detached or semi-detached piece of rock. Feel for even slight vibrations or movements of hand and footholds.

These techniques burned like a red-hot cattle brand in my brain by the time I ventured onto the steep and rotten limestone faces of the Canadian Rockies. I became so comfortable on loose rock that some of my climbing partners had quiet suspicions that I actually liked loose rock. Sheepishly, I had to admit that I enjoyed the mastery it required. I tap a suspect flake with the palm of my hand. It reverberates with a hollow echo. Loose rock is tricky even with the rope on. You always have to be careful while clearing loose rock not to hit your partner or the ropes. Over the years I had hit both: My partners never seriously, the ropes often catastrophically. I had destroyed hundreds of feet of rope at one time or another. Of course, misjudging a suspect hold could also cause a fall. In this case, if a hold broke I'd probably be killed. Yeah, that would be great, falling off and smashing body parts but not fatally, only to tumble into the river and drown with a freaking kayak tied to my waist. The coroner would have a puzzling time figuring that one out.

I toss off a few flakes and clean some dirt from the holds and continue up to the ledge. Making full use of the tree, I lumber up into a nice comfy slot between it and the cliff. I even have a couple of feet of rope left. Oh how I love it when a plan comes together! Throwing the short loop of rope left around my waist, I begin hauling and body-belaying the kayak up to my perch. Jim had taught me the body belay. Few climbers today have even heard of a body belay where you place the rope around your waist or under your buttocks depending on the aspect. As beginners we all became very proficient at body belaying. Even though I use a stitch plate for most belaying situations today, I often use a body belay for giving a partner a quick rope up a short section or if the rest of the gear is still in the pack. I had always considered it a valuable technique to know as a backup.

The boat comes up nicely. The rock is steep and smooth so the boat saunters up the pitch almost like it was designed for the purpose. Soon I have a grip on the bow.

"Okay, don't drop it," I whisper to myself, "or it could easily rip me from my nest."

I wrestle the kayak in behind the tree and it appears to nestle perfectly, balanced again, bow up to give those extra few feet of rope. The spruce branches even give a kind of spot to the boat, as they gently touch and caress the upper half of the kayak.

As I stack the rope so it will run easily from behind the tree, I stare back down to my launching pad of boulders at the river's edge. If the kayak slips from its perch while I am climbing, the boat will plummet, picking up velocity and momentum as it falls. When the rope tied to my waist comes tight, there is little hope that my fingers placed on even the biggest of handholds will withstand such a force. The stampede clowns, hearing my thought, turn and with raised eyebrows and dilated pupils begin licking their lips expectantly. They know there is potential for me to be ripped from my holds and be hurtled into the water along with the boat. The boat might just have another chance at being "The Bull."

This, though, is a very untypical climbing scenario. I need to bring the rope up because I will use it to haul up the boat. In fact, the usual safety that is created by the rope is now a liability. I need some way to jettison the rope and my connection to it in the event that the kayak begins to teeter from its perch. There will not be much advance warning; I will be too engrossed in the climbing moves above. It is almost as though I am climbing with no gear above a belay tied to a psychotic partner who might just leap off the cliff.

And then I have a recollection. I was in the process of rope-soloing a new route on the south face of Mount Fable and had started up the first scrambling below the face, but had not yet put the rope on. After 300 feet, the climbing quickly became more difficult and I found myself at a stance below a series of awkward moves. The pack kept throwing me off balance. I did not want to put the rope on yet, because above these six or seven moves the climbing would get easier. I could set up my first belay about 100 feet higher. If I stopped and put in a station, it would add an hour to my day just in the added rope work alone. So I down-climbed to a very small ledge about five inches wide, gingerly removed the rope from the pack and uncoiled it. I tied one end to the pack and delicately balanced the pack on the small ledge. As I made initial motions to tie into the rope, I noticed the pack shift slightly on the ledge ... If the pack, full of all my rock gear, clothes and water fell off the ledge it would pull me off. I could set an anchor and clip the pack in, but that would mean I would have to come back to this stance to retrieve it and again waste precious time. The position was identical to the one that I now find myself in. Only in this case it is not a pack that needs to be hauled up, it is a kayak!

After a few moments of reflection I untie the rope around my waist and place the end in my teeth. The other end remains tied to the boat. Wiping some sap off my hands, I begin climbing. It's a bit awkward. The rock remains vertical, so I stem against the tree for a few moves.

"Okay Stevie, this is the real thing here."

I smear the rubber of one neoprene booty on a small dish and wipe pine needles off the sole of my other booty on the pant leg of my wet suit. I glance down. The kayak appears solidly in its perch, even after the tree flexes a bit under my body weight. The river's whitewater trundles along 50 feet below.

"Not a good place to fall."

I make a committing move from my stem against the tree onto the wall and begin padding and laybacking on solid holds. This is the kind of situation that I used to love as a climber; a very serious position where mastery of the craft is quintessential, a calm and focused approach paramount. The sequences are long but comfortable. I am exposed for feet at a time, but edges appear as if out of the mist when I need them most. For a moment I am not of this world. It's like I am gaming with Peter at the Pearly Gates. We both know the outcome, but it's kind of fun inflaming each other's mastery. Peter feigns affability and with a chuckle opens the gate, but quickly morphs it into the gate of The Bull's chute. A twinkle. A taunt. He is teasing me! The misty ether retreats and the last shimmer of Peter's eyes turns into the glint off a large quartz crystal six inches away from my dilated pupils.

After 30 feet I pad my way onto a kind of exit ramp. The angle eases and I am out of rope. I have about 10 more feet of scrambling to go before I can reach the rim. The rock is covered with leaves and moss in many places. I know not to let the angle fool me. Leaves and moss can be like ice on a bobsled track. The footing is awkward and the balance too delicate to attempt to try to pull the boat up here. A slip would be cataclysmic. With the rope still in my teeth, I move up as high as the rope will allow. I kick moss and leaves off my footholds and unearth a jug for my left hand. I am in a kind of Charlie Chaplin crouch, my legs bent and splayed outward, my left hand outstretched. Grasping the rope in my right hand, I can feel the tension on it as it comes tight against the bow of the boat. I straighten out my legs and press my right hand up. Far below I can hear a muffled jostling as the boat quivers, then begins to slide along the rock, leaving its perch. I am now holding the weight of the kayak in my right hand. I am grateful for the friction over the lip at the top of the cliff. The palm of my hand rests on a small flat hold. I clear away more leaves and moss with the toes of my windsurfing booties. They seem to be gripping quite well on the damp rock. There again, I guess they are designed to stick to wet surfaces. And I am getting good surface contact, even if I have no edging ability. Once my feet are solid, my left hand leaves the security of the jug to reach up and clear off another reasonable handhold-anchor. I repeat the Charlie Chaplin shuffle and again lug the boat up with my right hand as I go. I am thankful to nature for providing me with purchase on this desperate exit.

Soon I am standing on level ground with two stout trees between the abyss and me. I hand-over-hand the kayak up the rest of cliff.

It is early afternoon and I still have a few more hours with the boat, but I've had enough. I return the kayak and the broken paddle with a deep apology. The proprietor behind the counter waves me off as though paddles break all the time, and he doesn't bother to inspect the boat for dents or scratches. Curiously, he will not look me in the eye. As I turn to leave the rental shop I notice a battered orange barrel in the corner with odd padding inside it. It is dripping wet. Turning, my eyes wide, I see the proprietor shuffle into the back room. Just as he is disappearing from my view, I glimpse a smudge of white substance behind his ears and on the back of his neck …

# Interlude in South America
## 1996-1997

These are stories from a windsurfing/climbing/ snowboarding trip that I took with my girlfriend (now my wife) in South America. I had planned on making a first descent or two via snowboard of the Venezuelan and Ecuadorian volcanoes. As you will see, I underestimated the risks as well as my own ability. As well, a significant part of the challenge was coping with cultural differences.

# Bienvenido a Venezuela
# (Welcome to Venezuela)

It starts when we arrive in Caracas. We have 500 pounds of gear with us, including the two windsurf boards, two sets of masts and booms, five sails, a mountaineering tent, ice axes, crampons, double ropes, full rock gear and my snowboard.

"Where do we pick up oversize luggage?" we manage to get across with our pidgin Spanish.

The airport attendant struggles to tell us in English, "It comes out with the other baggage."

I can't believe that our 9 foot 6 inch, 200 pound windsurfing board bag is going to come out on the conveyor belt, so we find a second opinion: Same answer. Karen and I are ushered over to the conveyor belts and HOOOOLLLLLYYYYY! Here comes our board bag out of the ceiling and down the conveyor belt. Leaving Karen to watch the packs, I rush over and manhandle it off the ramp as more luggage begins stacking up behind it. The huge bag will not make it around the corner onto the carousel without my coaxing. I shuffle the board bag off beside Karen — and here comes the sail bag, only eight feet long but weighing 150 pounds. I am getting a workout.

Finally we have all our gear in one spot beside us. We haven't moved 20 feet and I'm sweating already. Karen and I shoulder our packs (about 75 pounds each) and like a rickshaw driver pick up the end of the board bag in one hand and the sail bag in the other, with Karen and I at opposite ends. We shuffle along like slaves in the movie *The Ten Commandments*. Karen is managing her share of the load that is almost twice her body weight. I wince as I stare at her shoulders under the strain. I'm gripped that her arms are going to get ripped from their sockets under the pure gravitational pull of the gear. Somehow we make it through customs.

The last exit into the main airport is a sharp right turn that features a railing with horizontal bars. The board bag is too long to make the turn. The airport is jammed. People in the corridor behind us begin getting agitated. The noise level is that of a playoff hockey

72

game in overtime. Quickly, with no words exchanged, many pairs of hands reach through the bars of the railings and grab the board bag. We allow this to occur with the pressure mounting behind us, but then have a sinking feeling: What did we just do? We have just put half our gear into unknown hands in Caracus airport — exactly what our tour book said not to do — and we have only been here 20 minutes! We still have to get around the maze of railings. I holler to Karen to keep an eye out while I struggle to get around the obstacle and get my hands back on our equipment.

Again we manage to get our gear and ourselves in one place. We still have to purchase our tickets for the following day and get ourselves and our gear to a hotel. I haven't seen such confusion in an airport before: There is a sea of people. And the noise level is such that Karen and I need to yell to hear each other. All the signs are in Spanish and nobody speaks English. By now I am pouring sweat in the 100 per cent humidity and resign myself to the fact that with my hands carrying our rickshaw load I will not be wiping my brow every minute. I am starting to feel a touch of stress when out of the confusion a voice says in English, "Do you need some help?"

I do not hesitate. There is no question that we do need help. I answer quite loudly and with emphasis "Yes," thinking, of course, that I am merely answering a question. Well, before I can take another breath, the board bag and sail bag are whisked onto dollies and I am asked if I want my pack handled. These guys at least have official-looking airport ID badges on.

"Avensa, Avensa" I say, which is the airline we are to fly on the next day and the two men with the dollies start walking toward the outside exit.

"Whoa whoa!" (in the universal language) "where are you going?"

The English-speaking man explains that Avensa is at the Aeropuerto Nacional and is a short distance from here. As the five of us walk, I ask, "so do you guys just do this for free because there is no other transport between the two airports?"

"Oh no, you must pay these two men five dollars each." I almost start laughing. Well, I guess we walked into that one with our eyes wide open. And Karen makes it clear that for 10 bucks it is worth it. The other airport is about a kilometre away.

As we amble along, the English-speaking fellow tells of a hotel he knows of close by. "How much?"

"I don't know."

"Ah, so you know of a hotel close by, but you don't know how much it costs."

At this point we arrive at the Avensa terminal and are instantly surrounded by six taxi drivers. The English-speaking fellow becomes the go-between for us and the taxi drivers. I leave Karen with the gear and after some ado manage to get our tickets for the following day.

When I return, Karen is laughing, "You should hear these guys, they have been arguing the whole time about our cab to Macuto. It's a riot!"

Okay. So Karen is taking this better than I am. There is much hand waving, pointing at the gear and exclaiming of "mucho grande."

Our entourage is now nine. We had read in our travel guide that the cab should cost about 7,000 Bolivares (about US $15.00 in 1996). They were asking for 20,000. I contemplate blowing them all off, including the porters, and starting from scratch. But we still have to get our 500 pounds of gear to the curb, at least, and we do need a cab.

Finally, I begin to get into the hang of this new haggling culture. I pull out my calculator to help me figure out exchange rates, give Karen a wink and say, "20,000 Bolivares?"

I clack clack clack on my calculator. "Mucho dinero Señor. 7,000 Bolivares para un taxi a Macuto."

He throws his hands in the air and says, "Para taxi, sí" and points to the gear, "Para camión (truck) es 20,000!"

I happened to understand the word "camión" from my high school French (there are many similarities between the two languages) and start laughing out loud. Karen and I make eye contact and silently agree that we will not accept their price, but the taxi drivers mistake our non-verbal exchange as acceptance and immediately two guys grab the gear and began to load it on a taxi!

"Whoa, no no no!" They stop and give us a confused look. After five more minutes of back and forth — me clack clacking on my calculator — there is a flurry of hand waving culminating in one of the drivers making a loud proclamation to Mother Mary, storming off, slamming the door of his cab and driving away. No one else seems to notice. It is all part of the show. We manage to get them down to 10,000 Bolivares, but are still holding out for the 7,000.

While all this is happening, Karen pays off the porters and asks the English-speaking fellow, who is still "helping," how he makes his money. It becomes clear that he makes his cut from tips based on what he can get the other drivers for payment. Our eyebrows rise and we can't help but chuckle quietly to ourselves at the now evident conflict of interest our so-called mediator is in.

There are still five cab drivers left. Then another cab driver pulls up right in front of the gear and rolls his window down: "15,000 Bolivares."

I yell back in English, "You're not even low bidder!"

He counters, "7,000 Bs ."

Thinking quickly, I reply in pidgin Spanish, "6,000 for this trip and 6,000 for the trip back to the airport in the morning, 12,000 in total." And he agrees!

We load the gear into the trunk, back seat and onto the roof of his cab. We had anticipated this and had brought ample tie-down straps. As we pile into the cab next to the gear, Karen and I are quite delighted at our new-found haggling skills. We have managed to get them down from 10,000 to 6,000 — that's a saving of US $8.00!

The next day we arrive in Coro. The bus system will not handle our large bags. We need a cab to make a 70-kilometre trip from Coro to Adicora — our windsurfing destination. There is only one cab driver inside the airport. It takes us a while for him to understand where we are going. We keep repeating "Adeeecora," but he just looks at us with a confused blank stare. Finally, I pull out our guidebook and point to it on a small map.

"Oh Adí-cora,'" he says.

We explain that the gear can be tied onto the roof. He attempts to lift the board bag, grimaces, walks away and does not come back.

Coro airport is small. It does not take long to get outside. The one and only cab driver is across the street, leaning up against his cab and looking pretty confident.

"How much to Adícora?" I ask.

"15,000 Bolivares."

So in my crude Spanish I explain that I could rent a vehicle for the day for 20,000 Bolivares. He responds that his gas is too expensive for him to be able to do it any cheaper, and besides, our gear will not fit on the bus. We counter with 10,000 Bolivares.

He declines. "12,000."

Hmmm. What we need here is some good old-fashioned competition, but there are no other cab drivers around. Karen returns inside the airport and asks an elderly cleaning lady where we might find another taxi. The woman points across the street to the cabbie we were just talking to.

Karen responds, "No, otro taxi."

The woman's eyes go wide as she understands what Karen is asking for. She says a few words quickly to a young boy nearby.

The young boy looks at Karen, says, "Gringa," and with a wave of his hand motions Karen to follow him. I flash Karen a brief hesitant look. She acknowledges, but blows me off with a "I can handle myself" look as she follows the boy out of the airport grounds and into the busy street.

Karen later relays the following: "The kid flagged down three cabs within two minutes. He asked me how much I wanted to pay and he spoke to the drivers. For five minutes they spoke back and forth and they all agreed that a fourth driver, who was not there, should do it. And then, there he was — just happening by in his cab at that moment. They all yelled and the fourth fellow wheeled around, stopped and was informed by the others what we wanted."

Karen returns to the airport in the cab. She is jubilant and declares with the victory wave of a conquistador: "To Adícora: 10,000 Bolivares."

The car is a dilapidated Ford with a cracked windshield. It bounces like it has no shocks. Before we leave Coro the driver pulls over, gets out, pops the hood and adds a litre of oil. After all, it is going to be a 140-kilometre round trip.

After a few kilometres we are stopped at a military check-point by a kid who does not even look eighteen, armed with an automatic rifle. I am instantly concerned. The presence of the military is intimidating to us North Americans. But he just fans through our passports and waves us through.

Five minutes later we are on the road proper to Adícora. The car drives more like a yacht and constantly drifts left towards the centre line. The cabbie turns the steering wheel half a revolution until we start drifting back to the right. I am watching our driver steer in this manner with fascination when we pass a wrecked vehicle, black from fire, smashed almost beyond recognition and mounted on a steel pylon like a billboard 20 feet off the ground. I lean over to Karen, "Effective don't drink and drive sign." But by now I am second guessing the US $10 we were glad to save by hiring this ancient boat.

This cabbie drops us off in front of a hotel in Adícora. We pay him. As he is driving away, through his open window he says, "Bienvenido a Venezuela."

# Mailing a Letter in Punto Fijo

Did I mention that we brought our lap-top computer on the trip? Yes, along with our 498 pounds of climbing and windsurfing gear I threw in the lap top. I figured I would likely be able to scare up some freelance writing contracts along the way, publish a few articles and make a few bucks on our holiday. It would also come in handy for writing letters.

The process for getting a letter back to friends and family is always a science project: We take a floppy disk to Punto Fijo or Coro, both about 70 kilometres from where we are staying (an hour bus ride), locate a printer, print out copies of the files we want printed, purchase envelopes from the stationery store and then go to the post office. The printer, the envelope store and the post office are all about two kilometres away from each other. Not having a car means going on foot, or by bus or taxi.

In South America the operating hours at these places are never synchronized: The post office is usually closed between 12:00 a.m. and 2:00 p.m., the envelope store between 1:00 p.m. and 3:00 p.m. If you haven't started by 9:00 a.m., you might as well not even move until 2:00 p.m. because you'll end up getting stuck in the two-hour lunch break somewhere along the line. Two hours for lunch is standard in Venezuela and can be any time between 11:00 a.m. and 4:00 p.m. It can change from day to day.

Getting to the post office can't possibly be forecast because you never know when you are going to have all your other ducks in a row. It is rare that you will be able to do it all in a day, so you end up carrying your discs with you everywhere and when you do find a printer, you've forgotten to bring the envelopes and its a four-kilometre walk to the envelope store and back to the post office. But that's OK because it's 3:00 p.m. anyway and by the time you walk all that way and actually get there the post office will be closed.

Of course, the one day you are organized, you get to the print shop at 11:00 a.m. and there has been a power failure, so their computer is down and they tell you to come back in half an hour. You try another printer location: "The computer is in the shop." A third: "The printer is not working." So you go back to the first place. It will only be another half hour so you go have a café con leche somewhere and return, but then it's lunchtime and they are closed until 2:00 p.m. No problem. You just accept it as part of the cultural experience and try to get the rest of your errands done in the stores that remain open, and you show up at 2:30 p.m. You know better than to show up right at 2:00 p.m. All is well: The power is on and they are open. And then the attendant somehow erases the file from your disc while trying to bring it up. It doesn't matter that you know that this is extremely difficult to achieve because the file is gone. So you put your envelopes back in the pack and get on the bus for your 70-kilometre ride back to the hotel, waving to the post office personnel as you pass by.

# Shipping in Puerto Caballo

We are pleasantly chuffed after seven weeks of short board wind-surfing in Adícora and head to Ecuador for some volcano climbing, snowboarding and touring. The windsurfing equipment, which comprises about half the weight of our gear, will be of no use to us in Ecuador. Our tickets have us flying out of Buenos Aires, so all we have to do is ship our windsurfing gear there and pick it up on our way through. I manage to contact a fellow by the name of Captain Lucasey who works at a shipping company in Puerto Caballo. He says we can ship the gear for US $200.

We hire a local named Alex, who speaks fluent English, Spanish and German, to drive us there in his truck for US $70.00. He informs us that we have to stop in Coro to go to the bank because the shipping place does not accept credit cards! At the first bank the ATM machine is not working. We approach one of the employees and he responds by holding his thumb and forefinger a centimetre apart. We have learned this is the universal Venezuelan hand sign for any amount of time between half an hour and two hours. We leave to try another bank. At the second one we are able to get our cash. Alex needs to be paid some cash on the way as he does not have enough for gas.

During the trip Alex tells us that he does not have a passport (it is in Caracas), his passport replacement papers are out of date, his driver's license is a fake and that the registration on his vehicle is still in the previous owner's name, so that if he has an accident it will be blamed on the registered owner!

When we arrive in Puerto Caballo it takes us an hour to find the right building. When you ask a Venezuelan for directions, you will get them even if the person has no idea of how to get to where you are going. In all, Alex stops in front of seven different buildings. With no free parking spots, he pulls his truck over onto the sidewalk, parting pedestrians like the bow wave of a barge cutting through small chop, parks it and then opens the hood so it looks like he has broken down. Meanwhile, Karen and I look around for the shipping place. At one point Alex's truck actually breaks down and he has to open the hood for real.

Finally we find the place and the elusive Captain Lucasey. He looks at us in surprise, "I didn't know you were coming today."

"Did I not tell you on the phone last week that I would be here?"

"Oh yeah, I forgot ... "

This is typical in Venezuela. For instance, I had previously planned an interview with an engineer for a story I was working on regarding the water supply for the Paraguana Peninsula. He was late, I thought. Four hours later I received a message that he would be coming the next day. Again he did not show up. He repeated this process the following day. I wrote him off and began trying to make plans to find another information source when he showed up unannounced one week later. There was no explanation, no apology. He arrived with a big warm smile ready to talk.

Realizing that blowing my stack at Captain Lucasey would effectively alienate the only person in the city who could help us I say, "So what would you suggest?"

He stickhandles for five minutes, not really saying anything. This is also common: "The Mañana Blow Off," meaning, "I don't want to deal with this today. Perhaps if I heel-drag enough it will just go away."

We have experienced this, so I know to be persistent. I repeat, "So what would you recommend for someone in our position?"

Finally he realizes that we will not be blown off easily and offers to help us. The science project begins. We need a customs broker. Captain Lucasey makes four or five phone calls. Of course, no one can be got a hold of on the phone. Finally he says, "Come with me," and we walk a few blocks to a customs broker's office. The guy is not there. After another hour of touring the city with Alex and Captain Lucasey we find another one. Things are looking up and Captain Lucasey leaves. The guy we have to talk to is at the bank, so we are told to wait another half hour. No problem. We are about to leave for a coffee when it is suddenly understood that we want to store our gear there before shipping. "Oh! I'm sorry, we can't guarantee that it will be safe."

This initiates a goose chase as we go to five more custom broker offices. By 4.30 p.m. we are still unsuccessful and all the offices are closing. We are learning not to get frustrated by this kind of scenario. Alex can't help us so he leaves. I look at Karen. We are both soaked with sweat in the 100 per cent humidity. "Coke?" She agrees and we find a shaded patio to have a break. Because you can't drink water from the taps in Venezuela, you end up drinking lots of soft drinks. They are always ice-cold and seem to have an added extra kick of carbon-dioxide. They are served in old-fashioned 10 ounce glass bottles with a bottle cap that I haven't seen since I was 10 years old.

We will spend the night in Puerto Caballo. The first hotel patron asks us if we want the room for an hour or for the night. It's OK to rent it for an hour, but if you want it for the night you have to wait to talk to the landlady. OK … The next place in our travel guidebook does not exist any more. The third place, after we stickhandle a place to store the gear for the night, shuffles us to the back. (Presumably the front rooms are reserved for one hour rentals!) Nearby we find a great North American Italian-style restaurant and have a fantastic meal of cold beer, tortellini, caesar salad and more cold beer. We pay a typical North American price for it, but at this point we do not care.

It's day two and we are on our own. We decide to retrace our steps and keep in mind that North American common sense does not work down here. We go back to Captain Lucasey's office.

"Things did not work out yesterday, what would you suggest?"

He sends us back to the first place. The bureaucrat is there and seems to think we need an address in Argentina to send out gear to. (Keep in mind 80 per cent of this is in Spanish.) I suggests he calls Captain Lucasey — he speaks English. The three of us end up walking back to Lucasey's office. Somehow Captain Lucasey works a small miracle. We hand over our gear and are informed that it will be treated with kid gloves and will travel on the bridge, with the captain of the ship to keep an eye on it!

# The Bus Ride to Mérida

The Venezuelan concept of theft is different from ours in a fundamental way. For example, if you leave your bag or pack unattended in a bus terminal and someone takes it, it is not considered stealing. It is considered you not paying attention. This concept of not paying attention at your peril comes in many forms.

We still have one big bag with the snowboard in it and are standing there in the pandemonium of the bus station in Puerto Caballo. The bus station dude, with one of the two bus drivers, says I need to pay 500 Bolivares more for the big bag (about US $1.00). Sure. I don't care. Just handle it.

So we get on the bus and I hand the driver a 2,000 Bs note. He disappears and comes back and hands me a 1,000 Bs note and walks away.

"Hey! Qinientos Bolivares (500 Bs)?"

He turns and waves me off. So I figure, oh he has gone to get change. We stop 10 minutes later and everyone gets off the bus to get food etc. As I pass the bus driver I say in Spanish, "you get change, yes, 500 Bs?" He nods.

We are getting back on the bus and I stop at the bus driver.

"Cinco cientos, por favor."

Then he says, "No. Mil. (1,000)."

There is a lineup behind me so I sit down in the bus driver's seat to let the people get by me and say, "Señor (and in Spanish), the man at the bus station said 500."

He says, "500 each."

"No" I said, "500 para todo. 500 por favor."

But he will not give it to me and gets back off the bus. I follow him and repeat in Spanish, "Señor, el hombre de autobus dice que el dinero equal qinientos Bolivares, and qinientos Bolivares equal cinco cientos Bolivares, no?"

No answer. This time I put my face right next to his. "Senor, quinientos equal cinco cientos, no?"

He looks at me and says, "sí."

"So," I say, holding out my hand, "cinco cientos por favor."

He walks away and mumbles something about the other bus driver. Instantly I am on him. Same story in Spanish, same response.

By now everyone is on the bus. It is running and ready to go. I am angry, but I don't have the vocabulary to verbal the guy. I look at him and say, "Tu pones advantage de mí! Usted take advantage de mí." And then all in English, "You take advantage of me!"

By now the guy is trying to close the door and I won't let him. I immediately consider pulling our stuff off the bus, but the tickets are paid for. So I step on the bus and it pulls away. I stand there and now everyone is listening in the front half of the bus.

"Señor, cinco cientos por favor! I repeat in Spanish/English. "Usted take advantage de mí. No gusta (I don't like it). No gusta senor." And I look at both drivers and repeat loudly, "No gusta! No gusta! Usted take advantage de mí!"

And then I get an idea. "Cómo se llama su supervisor? (what is your supervisor's name?)" And I repeat it.

He says, "No entiendo (I don't understand)."

I look at him, "Tú entiendes. Cómo se llama sus supervisor?"

And then I get another idea, "De nada su supervisor, cómo se llama? (never mind your supervisor, what is your name?)" and I grab his badge pinned to his sweater and bend over to look at it. At this point he pulls out the 500 and hands it to me.

"Gracias" I say and walk back to my seat where Karen has been waiting patiently. Yeah, I know, all for a buck …

As we get off the bus, the bus driver shakes my hand and with a smile says in English, "Much life!" You realize then that much of this is just a game to the Venezuelans, to see what they can get away with. They don't think they are stealing. They just think you an easy mark if you don't stand your ground or if you let them do whatever they want.


## Bolivar Guards His Ramparts


On our seaside deck in Adícora I flip through our Venezuela travel guide and see a picture of a mountain featuring a steep couloir on its west face. This is Pico Bolivar, named after Simon Bolivar who led Venezuela to independence when he liberated the country from Spanish rule in 1821. I have never heard of it. And just as surely that couloir has never been snowboarded. It turns out the mountain is a reasonably popular climb. With its height of 16,410 feet, I reason it should be a good introductory high altitude climb for Karen. And of course, wouldn't I just love to bag the first decent of the west face. "Karen? I have an idea … "

So we take the bus to Mérida, a nice mountain town that is Venezuela's Banff. From it you can see the summit of Pico Bolivar. We immediately start trying to get information on it, like permits, routes, etc. While doing this, a local guide offers to come with us if we pay for his food. We say we will think about it. We had planned to meet another fellow Calgarian, Mathew, whom we had met in Adícora while windsurfing. Mathew shows up a few days later and I explain the game plan: He is keen to climb the mountain. Since Mathew is coming, it makes sense to have the guide come along. Logistically it would be difficult for me to guide Karen and Mathew up the peak and still snowboard down the route. I want to do it safely and not have to climb the mountain twice.

We are worried that when we go to get the permit they might see the snowboard and not let us go. But we stickhandle that OK. José the guide sees the snow board when we are just leaving. "Qué es?" he asks. So I explain what I want to do. He nods his head slowly. Later he tells Mathew he has never seen one before.

The first day is a 5,000 foot elevation gain. We have been at sea level for six weeks. Never mind that, I haven't had a pack on this heavy for years! Well into the day I am convinced I am suffering more than anyone else. Half way up the trail, a party of French people passes us on their way down. At the time I have taken off my pack to get a drink. The last guy stops, looks me up and down, stares at the snowboard and then at me and says, "Poco nieve (little snow)."

I am hot, cranky at the pack and at the trail and feeling like hell. And now I have this little French fag telling me there is no snow up there. I want to say, "Have you ever heard of a ritual killing?" but instead I hoist my 70 pound pack on my back and growl, my eyes burning holes in his forehead. "Yo miro (I look)."

He struts away and says, "Bonne chance!" with typical French arrogance.

"Wanker!" I think.

We arrive at a mountain farmhouse where we will spend our first night. It is a B & B — Bed with Bugs. You have to pay extra for breakfast. The kitchen has an open fire and no chimney, just a hole in the roof like an Indian longhouse. The room is filled with smoke, yet these people and their kids cook, eat and live here. Karen and I have seen nothing like it before. It is in stark contrast to our North American concern about second-hand smoke, externally-ventilated smoking rooms and bylaws that restrict children from smoking areas.

The second day is a 2,000 foot elevation gain to a height of 13,000 feet. I felt marginally better. Karen, however, wakes up feeling sick on the third morning. We've come too high too fast for her. Later she feels better. In the end we reduce her load and hike a ways to see how she feels, but after a kilometre she feels dizzy. We had talked to some guides back at the last camp and they had said they would take her down the trail if she was still feeling ill. Karen is really upset because she is so keen to keep going. We discuss it. I offer to go down with her. She suggests she go down with the guides and that I will see her in back in Mérida at our hotel.

I really have to think on this. The trail is an easy and well-travelled hiking trail. I know Mérida is very safe for tourists. We have a great hotel. People speak English, German and Spanish. I try to think about Karen's risk level with and without me: That of a lone blonde woman in a remote South American mountain area. Certainly higher without me. But by how much? The guides had seemed competent. If the guides had not been there I would have gone down with her, no question. But they were there. They had even set up a tent for her in the event that she did turn around. Finally I make her promise not to go down alone, to wait for the guides and not to go all the way down to Mérida in one day.

As it turns out, one of the guides keeps a real good eye on her and makes persistent advances! This is typical of the Venezuelan male in a society where machismo and sexism are palpable right from the basic family unit all the way up to the highest government levels. The dominant and ultra-conservative Catholic Church and its attitude towards women only exacerbates matters.

Mathew, José and I continue towards the upper, no longer in use teleferico station at around 15,500 feet. The trail is tricky, complex and dangerous in places. It is raining, snowing and there is a whiteout. I am glad Karen is not here. I am also glad to have José along. I would not have found the trail on my own in these conditions with the map that we have. Even in good conditions the map sucks and is not oriented to magnetic north.

As we continue into snow up to our ankles, the station still far away, I look at José and Mathew and say in my feigned French accent, "Poco nieve!" José and Mathew fall down laughing. It becomes the favorite line of the trip as we hike higher in the storm and the snow. Half hour later: "José, poco nieve!" Another gale of laughter. Mathew even starts to pick up some of my slang: "Wanker!"

When we arrive at the station I am feeling reasonably strong. After an hour or so, I strap on my snowboard and go for a run down the 35 degree couloir we had hiked up. It is a little intimidating being so out of breath. Obviously I am not acclimatised.

In the morning I feel terrible. I have a huge pounding headache and am on the verge of puking. I did not sleep well all night. It is still a whiteout outside and we cannot see the mountain. At noon I take some Tylenol and then sleep for two hours. When I awake I feel better and at four we decide to take some photos of me on the snowboard. At eight o'clock the headache is back. Two more Tylenol. We have the high altitude drug, Diamox, with us, but I have been hesitating to take it all day. Finally I pop my first diuretic pill. I am concerned about the medicinal illusion of feeling fine while unknowingly losing motor control, even slightly. I am aware that for extreme snowboarding on unknown terrain an acute level of precision is required in order to react instantaneously to changes in snow consistancy. In garden-variety mountaineering the world moves more slowly; you can stop and make decisions deliberately. Climbing back into my sleeping bag, I reserve judgement and decide to see how I feel in the morning.

I have a troubled and hallucinogenic sleep with crazy dreams about trying to ship windsurfing gear out of a port city in Columbia after dark! And then I realize that we have already shipped it in Puerto Caballo and that the gear I have is the gear I need. But now it is dark, no cabs around, not a hotel in sight and I standing on a seaside dock at night with all my stuff and the bandidos are closing in … And then I wake up. For some reason I think there are two French guys after me, trying to steal my snowboard. Bastards! I fall back asleep and soon I am dressed, about to snowboard off the cliffs on the north side of the teleferico station … I am awake. Still in my sleeping bag. Now I am gripped. Should I tie a noose around my ankle with the climbing rope and tie the other end to one of the building support columns? I try to wake Mathew up to tell him to keep an eye on me. But he doesn't hear me. At four a.m. I finally get a few hours of peace.

I feel OK in the morning, but visibility has decreased. Time to retreat. The two-day hike out is relatively uneventful.

I am surprised at my keenness for another attempt at Pico Bolivar. I have flashes of the same intensity I had felt in the old days on Highlander, East End Boys, the Golden Triangle, The Gambler and Windtower. I can hear the voices in my head, only ever a whisper. I have not heard them for a long time. Perhaps I will again have a few brief moments when the sword is once again free from the stone and I can breathe in an atmosphere of air and breathe out fire; be consumed with power; be free to tap into The Rage; be able to let loose without bondage; look over my shoulder without surprise when lightning strikes the rock wall behind and the clouds roar and scream, "May the real Steve De Maio please stand up!" It's the kind of fire in my chest that I hesitate to even talk about for fear of extinguishing it.

Karen and decide to return alone. But this time we will approach from the back side by Jeep, then by mule to the pass. I reason that if Karen can save her strength on the approach, she will have enough jam to continue up the rest of the "hill." In hindsight, somewhere I had forgotten about basic acclimatization practices. I should have known that ascending 10,000 feet in a few days would hurt us.

Hurdle number one is to get past the Inparques (Park Service). They do not allow you to go up Pico Bolivar or Pico Espejo without a guide. So we have to lie and tell them we are just going hiking. The Inparques dude asks about the snowboard. A fellow travelling with us tells them we are going to sell it at Los Nevados. Quick thinking on his part. (The ice axes were hidden.)

The Jeep ride is five hours long and an adventure in itself, our lives totally in the hands of our driver. For many kilometres the road is not much more than a wide game trail. The tires are literally inches from steep cliffs for much of the way. If we go over it will be chop cards for sure. The ride is physically strenuous enough for me to think that older people might not be able to handle it. Ironic for a Jeep ride. At one stop, a Venezuelan woman in another Jeep crosses herself as the Jeep continues onward! We actually see two wrecked hulks at the bottom of cliffs. But we rationalize that it is all within the allowable probabilities. How many car accidents had we passed on the highway? It's just that in our North American world the wreckage would have been cleared away. If they didn't the roads would be impassable.

Finally we arrive at Los Nevados, a little pueblo with whitewashed walls and red tile roofs. Situated on a steep hill, it is one of the most picturesque mountain villages we have visited. Even Jeeps can't climb to the upper pasados (motels). We manage to get our own little casa (house) for US $10.00. which includes dinner and breakfast. The owner is an older woman with golden-coloured, weathered skin. She is clad in earth-coloured clothes that look as if they have been lived in for a decade. When we ask for a private room, she asks me in Spanish if Karen is my girlfriend. I reply, "Mi esposa (my wife)."

She looks through me with knowing eyes and then mutters something in Spanish so fast that I do not understand it.

"No entiendo," I reply.

The guide with the other tourists interprets: "She says you are lying."

We all laugh and I say, "Coooomo? (Whaaaat?)."

Of course, when Karen tells her that she is a vegetarian and does not eat meat, the woman snaps back, again looking at me and in Spanish says, "Yeah right! What about him?"

Karen and I laugh out loud. Yes, it is clear by my size, particularly in comparison to the typical Venezuelan male, that I have not been raised on a vegetarian diet.

Renting three mules costs about US $10.00. One mule for each of us and one for the gear. The snowboard looks ridiculous strapped on top of the packs. The mule master has to adjust it so it doesn't whack the mule in the head as it flops up and down. The ride itself is a great way to hike! Same as the Jeep though. Just got to trust the mule. I keep saying to myself, "Don't fight him. Just let him walk. He doesn't want to go over the edge either. Move with him. You don't like to be disturbed on hard leads, so just leave the beast to his task." I cannot help, however, doing strategic fall planning: "Okay, if he goes now I have to twist off and push away so he doesn't land on me. And then I have to grab a shrub or an outcrop of rock ... Wait! I could tie the climbing rope to another mule, the other end around my waist and have a belay the whole way. In practice, however, this would be tough to implement. At one point I ease my concerns with, "How many mule carcasses have we seen at the bottom of any of these cliffs?"

By the end of the ride I am getting cocky and learning the Spanish mule commands and yelling along with the mule master: "Psst, chaaaar, haaah mulo! Psst, CHAAAAR, HAAAH MULO!" My imitations make the mule master chuckle as I tried to imitate him and we exchange smiles and nods as I look for approval and acknowledgement. It only fuels the perception of the other tourists that I am a nut case for bringing the snowboard. "Ah yes," I explain, "In Canada, it is considered a great compliment to be considered crazy. Many of us work hard at it. In fact the Canadian Indians say: "The so-called crazy warrior who listens to the voices in his head and lives by them is the warrior who becomes a legend."

We arrive at the pass. We have a 2,000 foot climb and a three-kilometre traverse to make. It is 2:00 p.m. We have five hours of daylight left and it has just started to rain. I know the terrain is tough. We will have to take the rope out at two spots for sure. Alternatively, we could descend 700 feet to another camp. It is up to me to make the call. Karen had a bit of a sore throat the night before, but says she now feels strong. I know she will not know how she really feels until we have been going for an hour or so. I decide we will hike to a subsidiary pass about an hour away to see how she is moving. It would be trivial to backtrack from there.

At the second pass I demand, "Okay, you have to be honest. Are you strong enough for four more hours? You have to tell me the truth." Of course, she is a tad insulted at this as I knew she would be. But I have to factor her responses in to my own assessment. How are your legs? Does your head hurt? Do you feel dizzy? I know she has never been to this altitude before. I also know that the bivy sites between here and the hut suck. If we carry on just one more hour on this trail it means we will either have to get to the hut or spend a miserable night out in the open. And if we bivy it means that Karen isn't moving well. However, she says she feels OK. She will just have to go slow because of the altitude. I know this is normal for everyone. If that is her only issue then I believe she can make it.

So we continue into the difficulties. The rain heightens and we are clagged in with visibility at less than 300 feet. And then we cross the invisible line where it is easier to go up than down. About 1,000 feet below the hut, at the end of the traverse, the sky clears and the sun comes out. "Yeah, yeah it's beautiful." But I can't enjoy it. The sun is low and I don't want to piss around in the dark looking for the hut, even though I have a compass bearing on it.

We are now above snow line. The snow is soft in places and we sink in up to our knees. I begin a steady monologue of curses: For the snow, my legs, my lungs and the approaching darkness. As we climb higher the snow gets harder and steepens to 30 degrees. Not real steep, but I yell back to Karen, "Do feel confident? If you slip you could go for a slide!" She reports that she feels good. I ascend another 150 feet and the slope steepens another five degrees. We are so close to the hut now. But my spider senses are tingling. I know Karen is digging deep. I, too, am experiencing high-level suffering under my pack. If I am hating it, Karen must be close to her psycho/physical limits.

Even though she feels confident, I know this is her first experience on this kind of terrain. She has skied steeper slopes. This, however, is not a ski hill. You need experience to know when you are secure. If she slips she might not have the strength to stop herself. Not to mention the rocks she might slide into. Not to mention I would have to find her in the dark and start a rescue. Not to mention … I begin uncoiling the rope and getting out the axes. Breathing heavily, I curse the tangles in the rope, the dark and the wind. The temperature has dropped suddenly. Karen catches up to me. "We are very close to the hut — I can almost taste it, but we're not going to have any epics here." And I give her a 30 second seminar on how to self arrest and use an ice axe. I feel much more comfortable having her on the rope. If she slips I am confident I can hold her. As I ascend I thread the rope through and around rock outcrops as natural anchors.

We arrive at the station, brew up, strip down and get in our sleeping bags. We are both cold and wet. By morning Karen is suffering badly from the altitude. All the acute symptoms. During the day all she can stomach is Kool-aid. I give her Tylenol and Diamox. She feels marginally better by nightfall, but still cannot eat.

In the morning she feels better. She is even hungry and manages to get some oatmeal down. Nevertheless, it is clear she does not have the acclimatization for the peak. I, on the other hand, feel good enough to go for the couloir. It is a clear day and the couloir beckons me. Even though it is late (9:00 a.m.), Karen suggests that I try to bag it. She will be fine.

As I'm preparing to leave the hut, Karen asks me what she should do if I take the big dive. Good question. We (I) decide that she is to do nothing but give instructions to any potential rescuers. She would have no business venturing onto terrain she knows nothing about. And she is not to try to go down alone, but to go down with the other climbers already at the hut. If others are available for a rescue, I explain that priority 1 is shelter: Sleeping bag, pad and stove with food. Priority 2: Get me to the hut. Priority 3: Get me down. I have not had to think in these terms for a long time. Karen, perhaps, has never had to consider such issues. Yet I have to rub my nose in it.

So off I go, snowboard strapped tight in the pack. To get to the couloir I was told I would have to rappel a short 60 degree rock band. I think, "Yeah, yeah, 60 degrees. I don't need a rope, I've been on overhanging rock thousands of feet high, climbed vertical ice. What can a little rock wall at such a childish angle do to me in a country where people don't even climb.? I was soon to find out.

I descend for 50 feet down the initial gully. It starts at 45 degrees. In the centre is a cylindrical tube of half-frozen snow about two and half feet in diameter and 15 feet long. I am sure that when frozen it is solid for crampons and tools. However, at mid morning it is of such a consistency that I envision it breaking loose under my weight. It would make a perfect toboggan, except that the rock below steepens to 60 degrees for 30 feet and then steepens further into an 85 degree wall for 40 feet that dumps into a chute that drops another 500 feet to the glacier below.

"Damn!" I downclimb, one hand on a rock hold, my axe in the toboggan of snow. Similar deal with the crampons. I am not a happy camper. I came to Venezuela to get away from situations like this. My head pounds; I am a little groggy with the altitude myself. Certainly alert enough for easy snow slopes but ... Suddenly, my crampon skids on the rock and teeters and the snowboard slaps the rock above me as I contort myself another move downward. Now I am off the snow toboggan and on the rock. The angle is definitely getting steeper and I begin to feel uneasy. Do I take my crampons off? I'd scamper down this in rock shoes (and without a 176-centimetre snowboard shifting position and throwing my balance off). My left crampon screeches as the steel gouges the rock. It is a bad placement. Belay with the hands! Belay with the hands! I test a large jug. It is loose. I glance down the gully. I don't like it. I make a move back left onto a small stance. Should I go back to the hut and get the rope? That would take another half hour and the snow would be that much softer. At least I'd rappel past the toboggan ...

The snowboard hits the wall above just to remind me of my position and what I've come here to do. Man, I want that couloir. The trophy of boarding it is blinding. So I take a dive. It's my call, like always. But now Karen is stuck and can't get down on her own. This is different. I blow it and I put her at risk. This is not fair in my book. By now my spider senses are raging. Air raid sirens scream in my ears. I am going to get beat by a piddling ass little mountain in Venezuela. I can't believe it. I am going to wank out. I glance back down the gully. This is nothing. How many thousands of feet of gully have I downclimbed? In a rare moment, shocking even to myself, I override my spider senses and my own psycho-physical analysis. I traverse back right and make two more moves down. The rock crumbles under my feet. Everything gets two shades brighter. My spider senses erupt like a volcano. For a second I am deafened by the sirens in my head. A kamikaze fighter plane explodes in flames in front of my eyes. I feel the pull of the void under my crampons. And then an invisible hand slaps me across the face. Snot and saliva are sprayed across my cheek and onto the rock. Suddenly I'm back. "You fucking asshole De Maio. What the fuck do you think you are doing? You get your fucking ass the fuck out of here." Ashamed of myself, I do.

I am pissed. It has been a long time since I put an effort like this into something and failed. I want to chuck the snowboard off the mountain and whale my crampon points into the wall of the hut.

But I don't. Instead I sit and stare at the wall for an hour. Karen watches and respectfully leaves me alone in my turmoil.

It is today or not. Tomorrow we will need all day to get down. I am shocked at how emotionally attached to the project I have become. The truth is I had underestimated the mountain on all fronts: The approach, the altitude, the difficulty. I had not considered fully the implications of bringing Karen up here. I could come back solo; take another five days over it. Am I prepared to get skunked a third time?

I have not drank from the bitter side of the cup of life for a long time. This is the black and white world. Not the gray of mediocre efforts and "impossible to fail" exploits. In academia and in most professional disciplines you can always get by and never have to accept failure. This, on the other hand, is the quintessential man against the mountain. And I had lost. In years past losing was just part of the process: Seven attempts at the north wall on Chinaman's, countless tries on Windtower. Why am I so trapped by this failure? Perhaps because I have been living in the world of gray for too long, a world where pats on the back are abundant, where wankers float to the top because they have "people skills" and someone gave them a life jacket. Here, only the cream floats to the top. There ain't no life-boats, no one standing on street corners indiscriminately distributing life-saving or life-making devices. It is mastery or naught. Perhaps I needed this to wake me up.

On the descent the next day, it seems to me that success or failure is not the point. The experience just was. Just is. It is part of the path. Part of my process. Whether I return or not, the experience is filed. All those who doubted and chuckled still will, regardless. It is boldness in action with total disregard for result which must be respected and held in esteem. Those other fuckers will politely clap their white-gloved hands from the stand in every arena, but never — ever — will drink from the cup. Only the bold will "Stand in there and take the hits," as my friend Bill Betts would say. When you are choosing between death and failure you can't hide. Speak honestly with the voices whispering in the back of your mind. Introduce yourself to yourself. Look yourself in the eye. Shake your own hand firmly. Yeah! Nice seeing you again Steve De Maio. It's been awhile.

# Cotopaxi:  In the Throne Room of the Mountain Thugs

I am psyched for an attempt at Cotopaxi, the second highest peak in Ecuador at 19,350 feet. You can get a lift to 15,000 feet and there is a hut at 15,750 feet. Perfect! We strategize that it would be best for me to summit first, try to board down, and then if Karen feels good with the altitude, I will go up with her the next day. Erroneously, I expect snow slopes similar to those on the volcanoes I had climbed in Mexico. On the approach, however, it becomes obvious that this is not a peak to solo. The whole mountain is riddled with crevasses. I suggest we summit first and the day after our climb and inspection I will make my attempt.

We are in the hut and Karen is feeling ill with the altitude. Several guided parties are heading off at 1:00 a.m. If I just wanted to climb the peak, I could try to hook up with one of them. But I think it might be an imposition if I wanted to be roped to them on the way down on my board! I contemplated a solo effort. It goes against all the rules. Karen might feel better tomorrow. Back to sleep.

Karen feels a bit better in the morning but is not having fun. I have to decide what to do. It is a solo effort or nothing. The route has lots of traffic, so there would be a quasi trail in the snow up there. It looks beautiful. I know it will go. But I hesitate because of the safety factor with the crevasses. I pace the hut. Soon my subconscious divides and there is a clone of me leaning against the wall at the window pointing at the peak.

"You know that its 99 per cent safe to go up there solo."

"Yeah I know. But it's that one percent that I am worried about."

"So, take the rope, two snow stakes and two screws. You can belay across the dicey bridges. No problem."

"Yeah, that's true, but this is not a rock climb, this is not Highlander. The crevasses that kill you are the ones you can't see."

"What? Those bridges will all be frozen when you pass them. And you could strap the board to yourself horizontally on the way up. It would catch before you plummeted any further. Shit, guys climbed it last night that have never had crampons on in their life before!"

"You know that is not the issue here. If I had to write an essay on what the right decision is, you know what it would be."

"Yeah, yeah, not to go. Looks like you brought your snowboard to South America for nothing."

"Fuck you!"

"No. The snowboard was a bad idea Steve. Everyone said it was. Especially if you wank out. Thirty-two years old. And a wanker."

"I am not a wanker."

"You are if you don't do it."

"I don't have to be that hard on myself."

"Yes you do. You live in the world of Steve De Maio."

Pretty soon blows are being exchanged. It is like I am in the ring with Mike Tyson.

"Fuck you! If I tell any of my climbing buddies in Calgary that I climbed this thing and boarded down it without a rope on they would say I was stupid. If I blew into a hole, they would all say that I knew better than that."

"Yep. And if you go down without doing it, you might as well cut your board into little pieces and throw it into a crevasse. Ship your ice gear home and call bringing it all this way a workout. It's a lose-lose situation for you my friend. According to you you're stupid if you do it, according to me you're a wanker if you don't."

I can't believe that my instinct is wrong about the board.

"Look at it man. It's screaming for a descent. And you might get an article out of it. A real article. None of this namby-pamby engineering crap."

I look out the window. It is beautiful. It would be cool to publish a few boarding articles. And then from behind me, "Besides, you really haven't done anything worthwhile in what, six years? No, you weren't even fit then. Eight years. Windtower wasn't it? Before you became an academic, then professional fat-fucker and sold your soul to convention."

"Shut up! I wanted to finish my degree and work in my field. And you know as well as I do that boarding down this thing is not an issue to do with skill. I don't mind crazy if the so-called craziness can be managed with skill. But being stupid is an entirely another matter. Rolling the dice on a glacier everyone agrees is stupid."

"If that's the case, toss all your gear into a crevasse and call it quits. Bringing the board was a bad idea. You're an amateur and not a good one. Your vision ends here. If you walk down this hill without doing it you're admitting defeat. And you are not even making a mediocre effort. You're not even mediocre ... "

We stare at each other for a moment with hatred in our eyes. More blows are exchanged. My head pounds and I storm out of the hut. I cannot think clearly. I sit down with my back against the hut. The other Steve follows me out.

"You're in Ecuador. You spent a lot of money and time to get here. You just can't walk away like this. The snow line is close by. I can smell it."

"Look. This is the text-book way that guys get the chop. They take risks they normally wouldn't take at home in their backyard. You know that. You've written fucking articles on psycho/physical bullshit and managing objective crap!"

"So you should be qualified to make the call. Roll the dice for the glory. All the big boys do it. Roll the dice this once. You know that chances are it will all be fine. You'll have bagged your descent and might even be content ... for a while. Whatever happened to 'The Rage?' Drink from the cup man."

"Cup my ass! You know as well as I do that Dougal Haston died extreme skiing in Switzerland."

"Yeah, but his close friends think it was suicide and that he skied down avalanche terrain on purpose because he was messed up after killing that kid when he was driving drunk."

"So what are you suggesting?"

He is stumped with that. He could not openly say that the project is worth dying for. I stand up and deliver one final blow that knocks us both down.

My ears ring. My head hurts. I will not go solo. I am shattered nevertheless. I stumble back into the hut and started packing to go down.

# Tungurahua: Should Be Good Training

Baños is a small town southeast of Quito at an altitude of 6,000 feet. Quite low. Travelling is hard work so we relax for a few days. We've got a great place to stay for US $8.00 per night. Everything in Baños is about half the price of Quito. Interesting, in that Baños is considered a tourist town.

For a change of pace I decide I would like to learn how to drive a motorcycle. As it turns out, anyone can rent one, even if you don't have a license. This is great news to me. I pay the proprietor of the rental shop and begin looking around for a helmet.

"Dónde es el ... " and using sign language I make a helmet out of my hands.

"No tengo. No es necesario (I don't have one. They are not required)."

I manage to get the bike into first gear and putt away around the corner before I attempt a shift into second. After a half hour I am confident enough to go pick up Karen. We do a tour of Baños and even venture out onto the main highway. We know that drivers in Ecuador are fast and by our standards unpredictable. It only takes 10 minutes on the highway for us to become sufficiently gripped to turn off and continue our ride through quieter residential neighborhoods.

Right outside of Baños is Mount Tungurahua (16,457 feet). I read that it has a snowcap, but no crevasse hazard. Sounds like a good snowboard exploit to me! Karen is a bit tired of puking in mountain huts, so we decide that I will take a look at it alone.

For three dollars I get a ride to an elevation of 9,000 feet. It's a further 3,000 foot-hike up to the hut (refugio). I get out of the truck and am about to strap the board on when this old guy grabs my pack and hoists it up.

"Hey! What are you doing?"

He explains in Spanish that I will need a horse for such a big pack.

"No no Señor."

"Sí. Es nesecario. Muy escarpado. (Yes, it's necessary, it's steep)."

I had been sitting around for a few days so I am keen for the workout, and mentally prepared to carry the pack. "Me gusta escarpado, Señor (I like it steep)."

He looks at me still holding the pack, "No no, es muy, muy escarpado." And then he mimics someone breathing heavily.

"Sí Señor. Me gusta."

"Es imposible!"

"Imposible? Yo quiero hacer un wager? (I want to make a wager?)." And then I laugh out loud. I don't know what the word for "wager" is, so I am not sure if he understands, but he puts the pack down.

The discrepancy between the relative wealth of a typical North American and the rural Ecuadorian is large. For this reason opportunism is manifest in situations like this where this man would have carried my pack up this trail with an elevation gain of 3,000 feet for only three or four dollars.

Slog slog slog to the hut. A couple of other tourists remark on the size of my pack. "No this isn't heavy, it's just poorly packed." I am actually travelling light: Clothes, sleeping bag, one ice axe, boots, crampons, camera, Walkman, snowboard and food. Half the weight is entertainment equipment! No rope, no crabs, slings or screws, no stove, no sleeping mat, no snow stakes or second ice axe and no tent. I'm not even taking water for this little stroll. One guy lifts it and says, "well that seems heavy to me!" And I explain with a chuckle, "It doesn't get any lighter than this! It only gets worse."

It starts to rain shortly after I arrive at the refugio. At 2:00 a.m. (the usual start time) it is still chucking it down. At 3:00 a.m. it is still raining, but the guided party are all getting ready to leave. I can tell the guides are not too happy at the prospect of slogging in the rain. Neither am I. But finally I decide I will go and have a look. Hike for a few hours and see if a miracle happens and it clears. My old pet peeve of getting psyched for a climb and having the weather turn, coupled with the last two failed efforts, spurs me into activity. It is a 4000 foot climb to the summit. By 4:00 a.m. it is still raining. I finish breakfast and think, "Well, I had better get going before common sense kicks in and I change my mind and go back to bed!" The other party is still eating. Part of my original plan was to follow the guided party so I would not lose the trail in the dark (another pet peeve). "Yeah, I am from Canada. In my country it would be rude for me to go first! After you, please." But they are taking too long. The guides are stalling. I recognize their expressions: "Another bloody miserable climb, we won't get to the top and we are going to get soaked!" I am sure the guides are pissed when I head out, because now they cannot make the call not to go; the other people have seen me leave!

The rain soon turns to sleet as I climb. But I have tunes on my Walkman and my sieve of a Gor-Tex jacket to comfort me in the small pool of light made by my headlamp. After 1,000 feet the sleet turns to snow. Soon I am hiking in five inches of new snow. Typically, I only put on my double boots when I absolutely have to, adhering to the old adage: "One pound on your feet is like ten on your back." Soon my feet are wet and cold. Okay, time for the big boots and the ice axe. Looking behind me, I am surprised to see the headlamps of the other party following.

I can just make out the light coming from the hut. So I take a compass bearing backwards from the first obvious rock outcrop. Twelve degrees. If it totally clags in I want to be able to find the hut again. The route description I had looked at showed a trend to the left from a "rock." But this outcrop turns out to be a spur that runs up into the mist above. Visibility is about 300 feet now with dawn having passed. One thousand feet higher, I take another compass bearing backwards along the spur. Interestingly, the spur runs exactly at 12 degrees also. So I continue climbing up the right-hand side of it, looking out left at every break in the rock. And then I see an outcrop, the biggest one yet. Maybe 40 feet high. If I have to give a label "rock" to a rock this is the best candidate I have yet seen. I skirt it to the left. Quite quickly the slope falls away into cliffs below, but there is a narrow foot ledge. Becoming skeptical, I go along the ledge for 45 feet to scope it. No. Forget it. I am going to trust my own route-finding instincts on this one. I downclimb back to the outcrop and start up the right-hand side. Now this makes more sense.

In the route description there is supposed to be a white cross at the end of the leftward trend. The crosses I had seen in the mountains of Venezuela were 30 feet high and could be seen from a kilometre away. I have given up on finding this cross. And then I climb over a rise and lying down on the scree, invisible until I am 10 feet away, is a small, three-foot long white cross. I cough out a laugh. Well I guess I'm on route!

From here I actually have to head right along a slight ridge to avoid a large amphitheater to the left. Bearing: 40 degrees. There is a snow slope to the right where the snow has drifted in. The rocks to the left are reasonably clean. At least I do not have to post hole. That slope to the right looks boardable …

Another 1,000 feet and I top off. There is a volcanic steam vent right there and no snow. It is warm at the vent, but also asphyxiating. To no avail I try to stand in the warmth and breathe in the fresh air blowing over the lip. I also try to take a few photographs, but the camera lens fogs instantly. The thick falling snow doesn't help either.

My foot prints into the crater are already filling in. I amble over to the edge and look down. "Okay Stevie, make the call: Do I attempt to board the slope or not?" I am concerned about the storm and the accumulation of snow. My mountain sense always says" Get down fast" during storms. How much longer will it take to remove my boots, strap the board on, board and then put my boots back on? Twenty minutes? Can I justify to myself not attempting to board the slope? On the other hand, I have carried the board on my back over 7,000 feet in the last 21 hours. I feel strong. My muscle control is good. Lungs OK. I'd have to keep just left of the rocks so as to avoid the cliffs on the left and not miss my turn off to the white cross. I quaff some orange drink and pause to think. Another two minutes pass. It is one of the those situations where the line is very fine and hard to see. I am cognizant that unknown to me I have already crossed that line, and that deciding to even think about boarding the slope is a classic example of "Escalating Commitment." Every M.B.A. student knows escalating commitment leads not just to failure, but to "Catastrophic Failure." But to me it seems the scale is in perfect balance. It will not tip either way.

I take one more look over the edge and convince myself to at least rub my nose in it. I walk back to my pack and un-strap the board. Boots off. Board and pack on. Ice axe in hand, I sideslip tentatively on the board's steel edge out onto the slope. The snow is heavy but soft. The board sinks to the bottom and I hear rocks grating against steel, gouging the nylon base. When I am 50 feet down, the board has a mind of its own and nosedives into a lower level of crud. I lurch and loose my balance briefly as I hit an unseen rock. The snow consistency is one that I have never experienced before, either as a climber or as a boarder. I traverse out further to the left. Still crap. It is only then that I think again of the steam vent. Is it possible that the whole slope underneath is warm? The lower levels could be in some form of advanced decay because of the heat. Hmmm ... New snow on ball bearings. That would tend to increase the probability of sloughs.

As I make further futile attempts to descend, I become concerned about my board stalling in the "quicksand" and then doing a header down the steep slopes to the left. There would be no rescue up here. I look down into the void. The visibility has decreased. I can't see an outcrop that I saw from the crater just five minutes ago. The five ton weight drops into the "get the heck out of here" side of the scale, crushing the scale into small pieces at the same time.

I descend another 100 feet to a flat spot in the rocks that I had passed on the way up. Board off. Boots on. Board on pack. Rock and roll. My steps disturb the snow into snow balls that roll into larger ones until they disintegrate, the classic symptom of a slope about to slide. Thankfully, the descent is uneventful.

# Getting and Keeping Money in Quito

I have to confess I am on my way to the bank machine alone, so I am breaking one of our rules. We had agreed we would only ever get cash from the machine when we are together. One person was to be the lookout while the other gets the cash. It is well known that you don't carry a wallet or purse in South America. If you do, it's a fake one that you have available to give to a mugger or thief. The cash you carry is generally split up into three or four different places on your body.

I notice these four guys eying me as I go in to make a withdrawal. I see them. They see me. I should have just turned around right then, but I don't. In hindsight, I can't help but think that my recent snow-boarding failures had something to do with me continuing through the first set of doors inside to where the bank machine is. The men are all little guys and have the audacity to follow me in. I put my card in the bank machine slot and begin my transaction. These four fellows stand at the other bank machine to my right and one begins to feign getting money out for himself. The other three are pacing like hyenas in front of their prey.

I have been back in Quito for five days working on a freelance piece and haven't had much exercise over the duration. For a few brief moments I want a confrontation. I want these guys to jump me so I can release some of my pent-up frustration on them. Finally I am at the stage where I am to push the green "accept" button for the amount I am withdrawing. My finger hovers over the button. I take another glance at my four adversaries. I am a big guy, they are little guys. And there are only four of them. I feel confident I can win and look forward to the challenge. I'd be facing overwhelming odds, but this just seems to fuel my rage. By now their eyes are on fire with the anticipation of a kill. Almost trembling in their glee.

The leader breaks the silence: "Hey, cómo está? (Hey, how are you doing?)."

He must have seen the glint in my eye and my jaw muscles twitching.

"Bien," I reply.

I turn and stare back at the green accept button. The green expands in front of my eyes and turns into a pack. A backpack. Karen's green backpack.

"Where are you from?" the leader of the group queries in Spanish.

Then I notice one of the others looking back through the glass doors with a curious expression on his face. He gives a subtle hand signal. The hair on my arms and neck bristles. The hazard is not all that meets my eye: There are more of them outside. The air raid siren goes off in my brain. There is a booming voice that screams, "Battle Stations!" I press the red cancel button and retrieve my card. I catch a glimpse of real disappointment in the faces of the four. They try to chat me up as I leave, presumably the "nice guys" decoy and stalling tactic. I walk out and they watch me for a block.

I shoulder check for the first two kilometres and begin to reflect. To survive a situation out of your control is OK. To provoke it is an entirely another matter. I am shocked at my behavior, but not so shocked. Mostly puzzled. Talk about risk ... in an unknown venue ... likely safer to board Cotopaxi without a rope on.

# Cotopaxi Part II

I have to have another attempt at Cotopaxi. I need a climbing partner as Karen has no further desire to hike up ski hills with a plastic bag over her head. We go to the South American Explorer's Club to pick up and send mail, and for me to look for a partner. Karen hears a fellow asking 20 questions about the route up Cotopaxi. She introduces herself and sends him over to talk to me.

Phil has just come from Peru where he climbed Alpamayo. I know of Alpamayo by its reputation as one of the most beautiful mountains in the world. He's young (23) and keen, and the idea of the snowboard does not faze him. "I just want to get to the top. I don't care how we get down!" He's my kind of guy. I quiz him a bit about his experience and figure he's got enough jam to get up and down Cotopaxi in reasonable security. At the very least I know he will be fitter than me.

Two days later we buzz off to the mountain. I give Phil a ten-minute seminar on crevasse rescue and at 2 a.m. we start the hike up the moraine below the glacier. It is clear with a three-quarter moon, so we dispense with the headlamps. The wind, however, is strong. It continually catches the board and periodically blows me down a step or two. So here we are, walking up this hill at night where the only real difficulty is the altitude and I'm getting blown down the hill! I do not feel as strong as I thought I would. I must have lost some of my acclimatization at Baños. Phil is stronger, having been trekking the last few weeks at altitudes of 11,000 - 14,000 feet.

At the toe of the glacier we put on crampons and the rope. I recall that one of my pet peeves on glacier terrain is having a partner who is faster than I am and having the rope constantly tug at my waist as I approach my anaerobic threshold. So I discreetly take the lead. At least there is some benefit to my experience.

We continue up the ski hill, plastic bags well in place. I think my plastic bag has a few less holes than Phil's. I don't mind telling you I am suffering. Step step step. I just cannot go fast. We pass one of the guided parties. Some consolation — they probably never had crampons on their feet in their lives before.

The first section is riddled with crevasses and much traversing is required to get around them. Luckily there is a hard-pack trail made by previous climbers. I make a mental note that I would not want to be crossing this terrain solo in the heat of the day when the snow bridges are soft. I had made the right call previously. At this time of night, although everything is frozen, there is no guarantee that every bridge will hold our weight.

Finally we pop over the shoulder below the final 600 foot climb to the summit. I have been buffeted by the wind for most of the way and have a headache. I can feel my coordination is altered slightly. Alpine ice glistens through the snow at the bottom of this final slope. It is also beat up by wind slab and is clearly not boardable. Time to drop the board. There is no point in carrying it to the summit.

I have a drink and something to eat and start up the slope to see how I feel. I tell Phil that if I begin to feel any worse he will have to stomp to the top on his own. But I feel OK on the final climb — relatively speaking. I am still sucking air like the intake on a V-12 engine, but my motor control does not deteriorate further. If anything, with the food and drink it improves. Of course, this may just have been me digging deeper.

Summit. Pictures. Then we piss off back down to my pack and the board. I feel OK, but know I don't have the jam to board the steep slopes below. I have managed away the objective hazards by coming with a partner. Now I am beat by my own purely subjective factors. I am disappointed but not overly so. Even with a rope on, this is mostly no fall terrain. Not overly steep, but hard-packed with coolers (crevasses) below some slopes. I am content with my judgment. I have made similar calls before. The plastic bag on my head is just a bit too snug-fitting for this terrain.

We descend several hundred feet onto a slight bench. This part of the slope is not steep and will be a great place to take some photographs. I do a quick calculation on time versus bridge solidity below. It is still freaking cold. Then I do a "next two hour weather forecast." There are broken clouds coming in and out but no precipitation presently. I am concerned at the prospect of precipitation and of losing the route on descent. Phil and I have some words. Twenty minutes shouldn't make a difference, so I strap on the board, make a few turns and he takes a few shots. I board close to the lip where the slope steepens. I stare down the slope, the prize only feet below the bottom of my board. This is as close as I'll get to my objective. It's unlikely I'll be back.

"You're not going to wank again are you?"

My head shoots around and there I am on a snowboard at the top of the difficult boarding.

"What? You didn't hear me? There it is Stevie. It's all there for the taking. First descent. Your first … "

I intervene in the conversation before it gets out of hand. "No. Sorry. This is a subjective call. And I have already made my decision. Nothing has changed in the last 10 minutes. This is just for a few photos."

The fight is over before it starts. Again, I am staring in the mirror at a climber/snowboarder who is not capable in his present state of managing the risks at hand. I am tempted, but we are still high on a big mountain. I need what I have left for getting down. I take the board off and strap it back on the pack.

By the time we get down, I am thrashed. I don't mind getting thrashed, but not when I don't expect it. I had figured we'd storm the thing. I have to say I am surprised.

Somewhere along the way I'd forgotten that bigger projects require a bigger dedication than I was willing to give at the time. I had underestimated the altitude and the difficulty. I had erroneously believed that I could take a novice to a summit and make a snowboard descent while listening to rock and roll on my Walkman. Wanting to tell a tall tale was not enough. These projects were for "men." And clearly I am just a "boy." Live and learn.

# Out of Retirement For a Spell
## 1997-2000

A flame is re-ignited for hard rock climbing. I also find I have a penchant for ultra-marathon adventures. Karen and I are married and shortly after our first child Stephanie is born, my perspective on risk is altered. For the first time I wear my seat belt while driving my truck to the corner store. It is unclear how this will impact on future adventures.

# The East End Boys

My '74 Nova roared as I raced down Macleod Trail, late on my way to the job site. While I drove I pulled my head, one arm and then the other through my paint-covered College Pro Painters T-shirt. My nostrils twitched at the odor of paint and sweat imbedded in the fabric. As I rolled down the window, the car's roar intensified and I made a mental note to buy some canned soup for dinner and to pick up some coat hangers. The soup tins and hangers would be useful for fixing the holes in my exhaust system. The suspension bottomed out hard when I hit a slight rise in the road. I cringed at the vibration in my feet as it hammered through the rusted steel floor. When the rattling subsided, I found I had to hold the steering wheel at a 90-degree angle to make the car go straight. No problem — just one more nuance.

A hundred and fifty feet further, the front end lurched upward until I could not see the road anymore. It came down in a nose dive, screeching and squealing as I skidded to a halt. Jumping out, I found the wheel on its side, wedged under the car. Hmmm. The ball joints had ripped out. I was going to be very late now. Rifling through my pack, I found my camera. Traffic backed up behind me. Setting the camera up on the nearby bridge, I crouched next to the wheel and posed smiling for several self-timer shots. A parade of frowning and agitated suit-and-tie guys wheeled around the bottleneck created by my photo shoot. As I ambled over to a pay phone to call a tow truck, I relived pitch 4 from our climb of Yamnuska's East End Boys the day before:

Near the top of the gently-impending crack, both fists began to creep out simultaneously. There was a reasonable jam down at the level of my shins. I knew that if I removed one of my two hands the other would pull. After a quick assessment of the situation, I decided my only option was to do a kind of downward lunge to the lower jam. I knew I would take a shorty onto the #4 Friend if I missed. I poised myself for the effort. My taped hands crept toward the outside of the crack half a millimeter at a time. I had only seconds to attempt this with any control.

"Watch us here, Bill!"

I went for it. And missed.

Bill recollects: "I felt the rope come tight and then go slack. I knew at that moment that the piece had pulled. I'd never seen anyone fall past me before and I braced myself to see it for the first time. I locked my eyes open and my hand on the Sticht plate. The rope came tight with a violence I didn't expect, and I was slammed upward against a small roof. Steve was upside down beside me. The gear clanked as he righted himself. My back was bleeding. Steve and I stared at each other. I had only known Steve for a week and was unsure how he would respond after an 80-foot screamer."

"You OK, Bill?"

"I'm OK. Are you OK?"

"I'm OK." I glanced down and unclipped the Friend from the rope at my waist. "The Friend pulled."

I glanced back up at the high point. "Guess I'd better get back up there before I get scared."

East End Boys. 5.11.A3: A quintessential creation from that era of my life. Right after the first ascent, I had wanted to go back and attempt a free ascent. For a few years I was distracted by other projects. Then in 1990 I more or less lost interest in hard climbing. The fire died and with it the passion for pushing my limits on rock.

In retrospect it was around that time that I became closed emotionally and my penchant for close relationships disappeared. Both are forms of passion that involve intimacy and risk. Shutting down emotionally and compartmentalizing pain, fear and insecurity became a crutch that helped me through some tough times. As much as I wanted my primal instincts to overwhelm my psyche and provide me with an intellectual, physical and emotional focus, they never returned. I would commit neither to a training regime for a climb, nor to an open and intimate relationship. It seemed I needed the escape route: That bolt I could lower off from at a moment's notice in case things did not work out. The issues for which I had created these crutches were long in the past. The crutches, however, remained. The skin on my hands was calloused. Under my arms it was raw. Where once they helped, now they hindered Like direct aid on very steep limestone, these crutches were not so easy to be rid of.

In January of '97, I found myself climbing recreationally in Thailand. I was doing more climbing than I had done since 1990. Daily I started thinking about the possibility of freeing East End Boys. I mentioned it to no one. My passion was delicate I knew. It was not possible to force it. However, if nurtured it might grow like a fragile plant. Or is passion just the physical manifestation of naivete and lack of judgment? Will a wise man never fully commit himself with no backup? Passion, almost by definition, implies commitment and risk. When I was a younger man I was passionate and committed in every aspect of my life. I took some big falls. Sometimes I got hurt. I learned to be risk-averse, conservative and closed. Was this wisdom? Or fear? Is this a wise man exercising good judgment, or drastically negating new life experiences? I did not have answers. But I could feel a desire welling within me. I chortled at the re-acquaintance, even though I feared another painful estrangement. Soon I would unveil the secrets that East End Boys had been keeping for over a decade.

By March I was back in Calgary. I bought a membership at the local sport gym and began silently training for East End Boys. My fitness level was terrible. I was 30 pounds heavier than I had been in '86. I rationalized this by convincing myself that I was just a "bigger" guy than I used to be. At the gym I ran into Andy Genereux. I knew Andy would be an excellent partner for East End Boys. I had climbed with him in '88 on the north face of Lougheed. He was tough, talented, and tenacious — a veritable climbing pit bull. The lead line, like a dog's leash, always strained for more rope as Andy practically dragged his partners up routes. He also was a big guy. Climbing with him I would get fewer comments regarding my own relative girth. I casually suggested that we go and have a look at freeing the route. Within weeks we were at the base for our first sniff.

The second bolt on pitch 2 seemed a long way off. I made two apprehensive moves towards it. My windbreaker chafed noisily on the rock as I shuffled into an awkward layback position. A snowflake melted on my glasses. I felt old. And fat. I was still 35 feet from the spot where I had used the one point of aid on this pitch. I whacked a small blade into a tight seam and pulled up on it to reach the bolt, muttering, "I've already free-climbed this part."

The crack in which I had placed a #2 Friend 11 years earlier was gone. The block forming one side of the crack had fallen away. I placed a #3 behind another block and gave it a cursory tug. The block shifted, then fell to the scree below, leaving the Friend in my hand. Hmmm ... Definitely looser than I remembered.

I managed to make a baby angle stick in some stacked blocks on the lip. In the '80s I would have run it out 30 feet on this piece. Now I was concerned that if I fell on it the blocks would pull loose and then land on me. I lowered off into swirling snowflakes and Andy pulled me in to the station.

With the rope clipped to my high point, Andy slung his battery-operated buddy over his shoulder and started up. The sound of the drill sent a jolt through my spine as if I were belaying from an electric chair. We were power drilling on East End Boys! Was I making a mistake? Power drills were now the norm for building routes top down and ground up. I could see how it would definitely make things safer: You could hang off face holds to drill, whereas in the '80s you had to hang off a hook in order to complete the same task. Ironically, having to place hooks in order to drill made running it out a safer option in many cases. In 1990, a bolt-drilling session on Quantum Leap during which I had hung from two hooks tied off in equal tension 30 feet off the station, above a leg-breaking ramp, in the dark, had coincided with my going into retirement. The power drill would have eliminated situations like that.

Andy finished the pitch and we rapped on one rope to the ground, landing at a point 25 feet out from the base of the wall. On our next effort I aided up the short bolt ladder, made a few more moves of aid above and hand-drilled a bolt. I had not expected to have to drill many more bolts on the route, so had left the power drill back in the car. I lowered off, cleaning a few flakes as I went, got rid of the rack and shook out for an attempt to free the bolt ladder while top-roped by the bolt above. This would be my first time rehearsing moves on Yam with a solely gymnastic focus. It was only a 15-foot overhanging section, but holds were conspicuous by their absence. Was this style an advancement, or a regression? It was certainly safer. As I rehearsed the moves, loose flakes broke off, changing the nature of the gymnastics required. The final sequence, once I had it figured out, involved a drop-knee at the roof lip, then a dead point to a sloper. I was quite proud of myself as I had only just recently learned the drop-knee technique, not to mention the terminology.

I carried on past the bolt ladder to terrain that I had free-climbed during the first ascent. A big, loose block formed another small over-hang above. The cracks were rotten, the sides crumbling slightly as I tapped in a wire with my hammer. I tapped in another and got a pin. All were barely better than body-weight placements. In the old days, stringing a pitch together with pro' that would only hold a slip was common. I mumbled my old adage: "If you don't put it in, it definitely won't hold."

I climbed up under the horrifying block. It was rotten, v-shaped, about the size of a microwave oven and wedged in a slot formed by the corner below. I had put a Friend behind that? Now I hardly wanted to touch it. I placed a body-weight stopper in a small crack in the corner below. Was I wiser now or just more timid? I weighted the wire and cleaned off bowl after bowl of limestone cornflakes from the block. I hung there. Another bolt? If I drilled it out to the right it would at least keep the ropes clear if the block cut loose. But that would be three bolts on a pitch that had originally been climbed without any — albeit by me. I wanted another bolt, but I was not particularly willing to give myself permission.

I glanced over and was startled by the sight of a set of crutches lean-ing in the corner. Beside them was a large fellow sitting in plain view in a wheelchair. He looked astonishingly familiar. His voice was husky as he said: "You're not as tough as you used to be, Steve. Two hundred pounds. Fat. Weak, physically and mentally. And now drilling on one of your greatest creations. This is akin to da Vinci spray-painting fluo-rescent orange on the Mona Lisa. Drill another bolt and you'll dream of the days when all you needed was a set of crutches. Face it; you can't handle it. You don't even trust yourself anymore, do you?"

The sun had gone again. Andy was patiently belaying below. I knew he would be frozen. Was I less of a man to want a bolt here? Eleven years ago I would not have entertained the idea — indeed, would have frowned upon it. I caressed the block with my hands. So innocent, but so potentially deadly. The man in the wheel chair grunted and we stared at each other for a while. He smiled when he realized I would not commit. He tilted his head back and cackled evilly because he knew that was why she had left. I felt cold sweat on my back. The rugosities in the limestone blurred into a placid grey. My fingers found the bolt kit. I could not ignore my intuition and experience.

Once the bolt was in, I felt drained. I watched a large snow-flake sink into my pile jacket like a hot-air balloon deflates into the grass.

"I'm thrashed, Andy."

"Whatever you want to do, man. It's a touch chilly."

"OK. Watch me here. I'm going to have one more solid look at it."

Soon I was struggling up the corner and onto the ledge. The Big Roof was 100 feet above me. I looked out left. Bill had been sitting right there when he held my 80 foot fall. I had landed down there beside him …

I ventured onto pitch 4 with some trepidation. This pitch had spanked me hard when I was at the top of my game. I climbed anxiously up to the off-hands crack and yelled down, "Hey, Andy, this is where I fell off last time."

Soon I was at the aid section right below the roof, spread-eagled in a big stem, staring at the single belay bolt on the wall. It was a tad rusty. I recalled arriving here over 4000 days before:

I placed seven small wires and clipped them all in to the rope in equal tension. Bill followed and took out the pro' in between renditions of "And there she was, just a walkin' down the street, singin' do wah diddy diddy dum diddy do … I'm hers, she's mine, wedding bells are going to chime." He would stop, look up and say, "Jimmy! Good lead Jimmy! This is the hardest fucking rock climb I've ever been on!" I appreciated his enthusiasm. It was also apparent that he was openly having fun while he was climbing. This was a new concept to me. Soon I was caught up in Bill's chortles, hoots and howls, in return calling him the affectionate "Jimmy." I enjoyed the light-heartedness in the face of adversity. Bill and I did not know each other well. We had only climbed together once before and only later did we each admit to wondering at the end of every pitch whether the other would want to retreat. The drive, however, was only upward. Unspoken between us was the shared feeling that the route was worth a bivouac if necessary.

Once the changeover was complete at the station, Bill looked at my seven wires and at the roof again, considering I am sure the 80-foot whipper I had taken not an hour earlier, and suggested that we drill a bolt. I was totally confident in the station and did not think that we needed one. I also did not want to waste the 15 minutes it would take to drill it. At the same time I was cognizant of the delicate nature of the climbing partnership, not to mention the fragile nature of the head-space required to climb on hard new ground. "Sure, Bill. If you want to."

Big Bill Betts blasted in the bolt in minutes. I watched as he took a quick draw, clipped the bolt with a seemingly exaggerated motion and then clipped the other 'biner directly to his harness. He looked at me and said, "I'm happy now!"

Bill recalls: "Yeah, and then you deftly and without any hesitation removed two of the wires and put them back on the rack! I couldn't say a word."

I clipped Bill's old bolt and placed a few wires. The station looked meagre, even with the bolt. "Andy, tie on the drill. I'm going to drill another bolt at this station."

Andy seconded the pitch, commenting that the climbing would be really good if he weren't so "farting gripped." At this belay we were about 40 feet out from the base with a 10 foot-high roof above our heads. His only comment as he climbed was about having to take out all my pro': "I'm thrashing my hands more than I would on a wall route." And then with a smile, "I'm going to take that hammer of yours away so you can't tap your wires in!"

"Well, Andy, experience has taught me that protection doesn't do you any good when it ends up dangling around your ankles, hanging from the rope at you waist after you fall off."

This had became part of our regular banter on the route. We both knew the potential consequences of the game we were playing.

Andy took a look at the station and said, "Usually I like to have three bolts at stations like this." As he racked up, I thought back to my lead around the roof:

"You're on belay, Jimmy."

"Cool man."

And I was off, tapping and tying off knife blades in behind expanding flakes and bottoming cracks. I had a rather crude system of aid in those days. Bill recalls: "You were probably the only guy who was strong enough to make your system work, but you made it work and you were fast at it."

At times the system involved having three or more 'biners clipped into one piece and alternately weighting each one. As a consequence, the 'biners would periodically hump around, making a sharp, snapping sound as they jockeyed for position. I was used to this. Bill was not. I could sense him flinching and locking off the rope every time the 'biners jumped.

I watched in fascination as Andy climbed. With the power drill he could tension off a piece below and reach to the limit of his extension in order to drill the next bolt. This was fully three feet higher than would have been possible from the same piece with a hand drill. Of course, from a bolt it was possible to top-step aggressively and even exert an outward force on the bolt as opposed to having to hang from a manky, tied-off blade placed behind suspect flakes. Andy was through this section in what seemed like minutes. I was startled by how easy the gun had made it.

Andy placed three bolts on the aid section. This was the one portion of the route where I had expected to add bolts. He then lowered down, dropped off the drill and prepared to try it free on a top rope.

I was concerned about the Big Roof. I had always thought this would be the crux. I knew everything else was free-climbable. But the Big Roof ... What if it was 5.13? Andy and I did not climb at that grade. If it was 5.13, then some stick man could come along and bag the free ascent. So it was in disbelief that I watched Andy effortlessly float up the pitch to the top bolt.

"Andy! How hard is it?"

"Well, it's a 5.8 or 5.11."

"Really? You ran up it!"

"Well, I knew where all the holds were. Some of the hollow flakes I knocked off left jugs underneath."

I was ecstatic. We had it. It was bagged. The hard climbing was over. Our next effort would cinch it. And the Big Roof was just a jug tug!

Soon we returned for the free attempt. The large fellow in the wheelchair followed close on my heels up the trail. This guy could get anywhere in that damned wheelchair. "You think you can climb two hard routes over two days on Yam? You're already tired, aren't you? Blew your wad yesterday and this climb is harder. And ... " He chuckled, popped a wheely in his chair, and balancing on two wheels made a quick spin while shrieking: "And you can't fall off today or hang. It doesn't count if you do." He continued his two-wheeled spin and began to chant like a little kid in time with his rotation: "You're going to hang, you're going to hang."

Andy was raring to go. He pegged the redpoint on pitch 2. To save my jam for the leads, I followed on jumars and rigged up for the 12a pitch. I got the micro hold, made the drop-knee, but blew off on the sloper. The man in the wheelchair squealed as the rope came tight, and grinned as he nudged the crutches in the corner a little closer to me. I hung, shook out and completed the pitch. Andy seconded flawlessly and fired up pitch 4. At the off-hands crack he greased off and took a shorty. He was back on instantly and sent the aid section to the station. I again followed on the jumars.

My friend in the chair was further delighted when I dogged my way over the Big Roof. At least it was only a 100 feet of 5.7 to the station, or so I recalled. I fought for a half-hour to get through a loose 5.10 section above the roof which completely took me by surprise. I had previously graded this section 5.7.

Pitch 6 was the last bit of aid yet to be freed. It was Andy's lead. I stared up at it as I belayed, and recalled:

I was getting tired and retorted to Bill, "Do you ever notice how the climb is never over when you want it to be?"

Bill chuckled. "What? Have you had enough?" as he grabbed the rack and started up the pitch. With no other protection in, Bill leapfrogged #4 Friends on aid up the wide, overhanging crack. I lay sprawled on the sloping ledge below. I started to attention when I heard the sound of a Friend ripping across limestone and the clatter of gear. As I looked up, my mind shot to the integrity of our belay station. A Friend had pulled and Bill had fallen onto the lower one, but the rope had not come tight. His cowtail sling had held the fall. Bill instantly plugged in the other Friend and quickly freeclimbed for another 30 feet to a ledge on the left, where he began ferreting out a station. The sound of iron on iron rang out into the afternoon as Big Bill Betts pounded in a solid belay. I jumared past the overhanging crack, racked up and continued to below another small roof.

"You know, Bill, every pitch on this route is either over-hanging or has an overhang on it."

Bill concurred as he directed my attention briefly to the bent carabiner on his harness: "I had to open the gate with my hammer … "

"Hey, Andy, get some gear in before the wide crack, will you."

Andy expertly manipulated the wide crack to his advantage. He was climbing strongly and with confidence as he gave me a full running commentary of the moves. For a brief instant it felt as it we were totally in control, just finishing off a fun-in-the-sun rock climb.

Andy's tone alerted me before I could comprehend the words. "Steve! Rock!"

A shower of toaster-sized howitzers filled the sky. I hugged the wall, still totally exposed, hunching my shoulders and bulldogging my neck. Crack! Thud! One on the helmet, one on the shoulder. I heard Andy's concerned voice as a background to the fireworks in front of my eyes. I shook my head and felt my shoulder and collarbone. Nothing broken. Just numb.

"I'm OK," and then to myself, "this is still a very serious game!"

By freeing all the moves, we had reduced the aid grading from A3 to A0 only, as each of us had taken hangs or falls on our respective hard pitches. We had to return for clean leads of these pitches in order to truly free climb the route.

A cloud of dust extended in a plume behind us as we drove into the Yam' parking lot. It was early and the parking lot was empty save for one person — the man in the wheelchair. He sat there waiting and glowered at me over his coffee mug. As we got out of the truck, he tossed a pair of crutches in my general direction. They fell to the ground with a clatter. "You don't feel good, do you? Mentally waxed? Emotionally drained? Things are not great at home right now, are they? You think you can redpoint a 5.12 pitch today?" He chortled: "You've never redpointed a 5.12 and you think you can pull it off three pitches off the deck on Yam'?" I squared off momentarily and prepared to butt heads, but then backed off. Save it for the route.

Andy resent pitch 2 in minutes. After following on the jumars, I quietly ate an Eatmore bar and had a drink as I selected the rack for pitch 3, the crux of the route: No hammer, no pins, a few wires and some bigger stuff for up high. I clipped the first bolts and then downclimbed back to the belay for a brief rest. I had rehearsed the moves in meditation over a 100 times in the prior week. In my mind I quietly repeated the mantra as I executed each move: "Begin with the two-finger layback to the sharp micro hold, then drop-knee and slap for the sloper. Got it. Okay, stay low on it so you don't barn door off." I brought my left foot above the roof and began to stand. The flake it was on snapped off, but my arms took the weight and I held on. I had nanoseconds to respond or I would be off. Andy pointed his finger like a pistol three inches from the rock and urgently yelled: "Foothold!" And just under the lip was a hidden foothold that I could not see. It made the difference. I armed my way up to the pseudo-rest. I had done it, finally pulled the crux without blowing off.

Now there was only the easy 5.11 section past the loose block. It went and soon I was clipping the belay bolts. I let out a howl. I hadn't let out a howl on the crag in a long time. The large man fidgeted in his chair.

Andy seconded, refusing the offer of the jumars. He fired his pitch to the Big Roof, this time bypassing the wide crack on some face holds on the right. Two redpoints down, one to go.

Now for the Big Roof. I made the moves past all three bolts and was into the overhanging flare above. There was a good stopper crack right in from of my nose. Do I stop and put one in, or do I keep going to the rest? My arms and legs burned from the contorted stem position. As I was getting arranged, my left hold blew. I swung right, but resisted with my stem.

"You alright?" I was out of Andy's view.

"Yeah! Hold popped but I didn't fall." The exposure pulled at my heels. My butt was now 50 feet out from the base of the wall. The rocks were landing outside the trail at the base.

I got the stopper in and climbed four feet higher. Only two more moves to the rest. Once again the rock on my left tore away in my hands. I was off. My legs swung wildly into space. But the hold on the right was good. I dug deep into my psyche: 11 years into the past, when I was an East End Wildboy; when the healthy dissatisfaction that I lived with daily spurred me on to bigger, better, and increasingly more improbably projects; when I roared on protectionless pitches and howled at the face of adversity. Momentarily I became that person again. The doors blew off every compartment I had ever created. My body pulsed as new blood surged. The crutches turned to ash in the corner. My feet darted to new positions. My eyes squinted, then focused like laser beams on the remaining holds, almost burning holes in the rock. The piece at my shins swung ever so gently. The man in the wheelchair stood up in disbelief.

A few moves higher at the rest I got some pro' in and quickly shrank back to my timid self. Slowly and methodically I made my way to the station. The man in the wheelchair sat back down, magically produced another pair of crutches and gently, tauntingly, placed them in the corner. Our eyes locked once more. I hissed, "Only if I need them, you bastard!"

East End Boys was free. Me? Well, I'm working on it ...

My 17 year-old Toyota Tercel roared down 16th Avenue towards downtown. My body had that pleasant soreness from the effort of the climb the day before. As I pulled over and stepped out to pick up some soup cans from a recycling box at the roadside, I realized that the suit I was wearing was worth more than the car. I ate out a lot and did not like canned soup anymore. I would, however, need these tins to cover the holes in my exhaust system. I tossed the shiny cans into the back with a clatter, readjusted my silk tie and buckled up. You never know when a wheel might fall off ...

# The East End Boys

I've got two fist jams.
One at face level.
One at chest.
Simultaneously
both begin to creep
out of the slippery crack.

Removing one
will cause the other
to surely pull.
Down at my shins
the crack narrows
to bomber hands.
Just have to get there.

If I blow
I'll take a shorty
onto number 4 Friend.
"Watch us here Bill."
Lunging downward
— I miss —
and plummet.

The rope jerks.
The Friend rips.
Eighty feet later
I'm upside-down
beside the belay.
Bill is launched
into an overlap.

Inverted I ask,
 "You OK Bill?"
"I'm OK."
"Are YOU OK?"
Still stunned:
"I'm OK. Are YOU OK?"
"Yeah. I'm OK."

Reaching for the rope
Between my legs,
I yard myself upright.
Apologetically,
"The friend pulled."
"Guess I better get back
Before I get scared."

Bill, swinging in space,
jumars and chortles
"OOOOEEEE Son!
This is the hardest
fucking rock climb
I have ever been on!"

Tentatively I ask,
"Have you done much aid?"
Bill looks up at the roof.
He looks straight down
To the scree,
my eighty-foot screamer
Still hot on his hands.

"Don't ask me that question
 NOW."

# Surfin' the Curve

Most of the time I don't see it coming, like an avalanche bludgeoning from a hidden bowl high on a steep face. For minutes at a time my brain is strapped solo on this climb, fighting the futility of all my existence, staring wide-eyed into the black abyss that is my life. There is a heightened awareness; a craving for understanding well beyond what is socially acceptable. Yet simultaneously, there is a need for an outlet of such scope that I am tortured by it. I am stranded in purgatory, craving a set of chin-ups that will trash me while I murmur my blackest, most depressing poetry. The people around me stand like lampposts, only further illuminating my desperation. I learned long ago that I can never communicate these sufferings. They are my yoke. Time to get out from under the lamplight and go home and deal with it. Walk out that door, Stevie. Go and find your way to channel it.

I manage to make my way back to my condo. Clothes fall into the washer. Food warms in the microwave. I sit aimlessly at my desk and shuffle paper. I cut a finger on one of the envelopes. A blotch of blood forms, then grows into a bubble, its surface under tension. I hold it up to my eyes. It breaks and streams down my hand. The bell rings on the microwave. The dishwasher shifts cycles and my eye catches the moon in the sky, poking around an illuminated cloud. I put my fingers in my mouth. Mmm … the acrid taste of blood. The white light expands into a white wall encompassing everything, then it cracks and the pieces begin to fall like giant chunks of brittle ice. A massive jigsaw puzzle crumbling before my eyes.

Soon these pieces pile up on my desk into a large mound of ice shards. In a trance I begin building a shape out of this pile of ice, melting this piece, joining that, until I can envision a physical and psychological sculpture. I am pleased with its form. I touch it, caress it, feel its energy. It screams for realization. I am intimate with its desire for manifestation in the real world: To be brushed in broad, harsh strokes on the canvas of reality.

It is not long before I have it. From out of this manic meditation my sculpture congeals into a healing vision: A "quadrathon" in the mountains. Begin by headlamp and climb the 1000 feet of north-facing ice on The Professor Falls. Drive over to Yamnuska and saunter up 700 feet of south-facing limestone. Rollerblade the 50 miles from Yam to Calgary, leap onto my bicycle and cycle the 50 miles back to pick up the truck — all of it solo.

Suddenly I am back at my desk. All the papers are on the floor. The moon is gone out of the window. My hair is damp with sweat. There are streaks of dried blood on my arm. My conscious mind hurls into the logistics of execution. I have joyed in many link-ups in the past, but this would be my most ambitious, most risky and likely most rewarding. The sheer craziness of it makes my spine tingle at the prospect: To tour-de-force on the tightrope, to dance on the high wire, in tension between endurance and speed. Each step subtle, yet distinct. Each touch gentle, yet severe. Every motion unknown, until made. I crane my neck and howl in anticipation of the adversity.

White again encompasses my world. A shard of brittle ice sails over my left shoulder. It is early and the ice is not yet plastic. I squint my eyes and hunch my shoulders, bracing at the sound of spindrift spilling over the lip above. There is, I know, a huge hidden bowl above the route. A white plume sugar-coats me with a dusting of powder snow. Sweat and spindrift-melt drips down my upper lip and into my mouth. I stare hard at the white curtain: A thousand tiny grey daggers hang from its every feature and point at me like so many sharks' teeth. I chant to myself: "White is ice," the ice of the final, crux pillar of Professor's. It is 8:45 a.m. Tap tap hook, tap tap hook. "White is ice; ice is nice." Tap tap hook to set, weight and breathe.

High over the lip of the pillar, a big black raven circles. For some reason, as I hang there breathing, this bird forces an instant of introspection: Do I seem absurd from his perspective? I don't seem absurd to me, but then I am intimate with this process. But I have to chuckle to myself. It did take me 30 odd years to understand it.

In the first decade of my life I recognized my propensity for adventure for its own sake. By the age of nine or ten this further metamorphosed into an attraction towards adventures that had some challenge associated with them. By 12 I knew I wanted to be a rock climber, and at 14 I was officially indoctrinated into the brotherhood. By my late teens the concept of risk analysis in the venues of adventure challenges was well ingrained. By my mid-20s I had a fairly well-developed understanding of my psychological and physical limitations, of objective and subjective risks and of my relative competence at any instant in time. By the age of 30 I began to study the peaks and valleys of my intellectual, physical and emotional states and how they affected my performance in gymnastic, endurance, artistic or cerebral exploits, both inside and outside of high-risk environments. Generally, the lows in the cycle were to be avoided.

I began to recognise swings in my nature in much more pragmatic ways. Mania and introspection were a part of my day-to-day existence. The amplitude and frequency of these cycles varied radically. I had become quite comfortable with my periods of mania and had learned how to exploit them. These moments were of such value that I coveted their arrival. On the other hand, introspection — which in those days I called depression — was socially unacceptable and was therefore to be avoided, and, above all, never to be discussed.

It wasn't until I was in my early 30s that I learned the value of these periods and consequently renamed them "introspection," a new label that helped remove the negative connotations. When a wave of introspection hit, I learned to encourage it by pursuing activities that were complemented by deep reflection like writing, painting or meditation. The challenge I uncovered was to not only exploit the highs, but to also exploit the lows, and if possible everything in between. I was learning to "surf the curve."

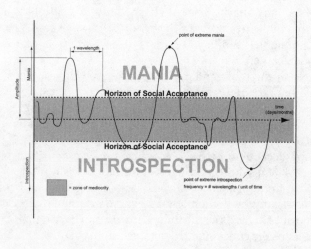

I hammer the adze with the palm of my hand and then give the shaft another hard yank. Levering the shaft prematurely pries off a small dinner plate with a hiss. It lands in the crook of my arm. Instinctively, I give my arm a wriggle and the ice slips easily away. The raven is still circling, watching. "What?" I say to him, "I told you it started when I was a child."

Mom says that when I was two years old I'd stretch and curl my fingers around the lip of the counter and then do a pull-up in order to see what was up there. The confines of my playpen presented only a minor obstacle and I was regularly up and over the rail and into an adventure with my older brothers and sister. Two years later, when I was four, I made a fateful attempt to follow my siblings into a very high tree fort. The crux move was a tricky traverse where the ladder went from one side of the tree to the other. Little Stevie got stuck right at mid crux — unable to go up or go down. Daddy heard my cries for help, plucked me off and carried me over his shoulder back down to the ground.

The bird seems to further question my rationale. He hovers momentarily in the updraft as if to say, "That's a simplification!" I turn back to the ice, but those black eyes burn holes in the back of my helmet. I didn't mean to suggest it was simple, easy or never-changing. The day I turned 35 another variable got added into my nicely quantified framework.

"The epidural is taking."

The fluid line dangles out of Karen's spine. She has been valiantly enduring labor for the last 30 hours, but has progressed very little. Her energy reserves are rapidly depleting. The midwives suggest drugs in order to give Karen some rest. We had aspired to a natural birth, but just over 60 minutes ago made the decision to intervene medically.

A nurse interrupts, "Baby's pulse has dropped to 80."

"Are we getting mother's heart rate on sonic? Or is that baby's?"

The nurses and midwives stare at each other.

"Put in the electronic."

There is a flurry of cables, wires and hands. I am pacing. I hope these people know what they are doing. Our baby's pulse has been steady at 130 throughout the last 30 hours; in fact, throughout Karen's pregnancy. Everyone's countenance has turned serious. The nurse's hands are a blur as she hastily tears off the Velcro on the sonic readout. I feel like we are unroped in a narrow ice gully and panicking to place our only ice screw before an avalanche hits. The digital readout is inserted. It is stuttering like there is a loose connection. This does not help my confidence level.

Another hook placement knocks a small ice chip into my eye. It stings. I hang there, my arms feeling the beginning of a gentle burn. Aggressively and rapidly, I open and close the eye, trying to melt and clear the ice. Suddenly ice cracks under my left crampon and a cauliflower head plummets 130 feet to the snow ledge below. It bounces once. The raven is gone.

"Baby's pulse is still 80. It's in distress. Take Karen to OR. We will recheck the pulse and C-section if it stays low."

Karen is whisked out of the room and down the hall ahead of me. A nurse blocks my entry into the operating room, asserting that I cannot enter without a sterile gown and booties. Through the still swinging doors I can hear the fear in Karen's voice demanding my presence. I want to knock this nurse down. At that moment an aid hands me a sterile outfit. Focus on getting the gown on. Booties over the shoes? They'll never fit over my Hi-Tecs. Shoes off now!

I would save only minutes. But minutes are minutes, especially when tallied under an expansive white blanket draped precariously in a steep-sided bowl. Topping off, I do not coil the rope. Rather, I trail my 8.5 mm behind me into the trees. I have never liked being exposed in the fall-line under avalanche terrain.

I recall vividly the day I found my very first rope. It was springtime and all the "big garbages" (as I called them) were out in front of all the houses. These always excited me as there was always neat stuff to be found by picking through the piles. On this particular day, I was on my two-wheeler making my rounds looking for an old broom, a rake or shovel handles. They made excellent swords or spears. Stopping at a "big garbage" just around the corner from our house, I looked more closely inside a cardboard box, gasped, and was off my bike in an instant. Reaching inside, I touched what appeared to be an old hemp cord. Weather-beaten brown, frayed over its length, it had a few knots in it and two cool, rusted iron clips attached to it. My heart raced. I bunched up the rope, and like a pirate with his treasure made my way back home. My little nine-year-old body tingled with the possibilities for adventure that this ratty piece of tat would allow.

Soon I am out of any potential avalanche's path and descend to a large tree. I thread a sling and toss the ends of my rope down the rock band. It is a 30-metre rappel. My doubled line is 25; I will have to be careful not to rap off the end of the rope. Maintaining my purchase on the rock, I let the ends slide through the descender. My crampons scrape white marks on the limestone and I momentarily use a much smaller pine tree growing out of the cliff face as a foothold. I smile to myself as I remember.

At the age of nine, I envisioned climbing all the trees on our street in a day. I grew up in Southern Ontario and our street was lined with mammoth maple trees, many of which had huge trunks. The arms of these great trees created a tunnel of leaves over the road in summertime. I remember joying in the strife as I pulled from one tree into the next, finally into the last one. I was trashed. My hands and little body smarted with muscle aches and abrasions. I was never able to replicate this feat again.

A few more short rock bands on the descent feature tree moves as I make my way back to the base of the route. After stuffing all the ice gear into my pack, I begin to jog back to the truck. The trail is a tad slippery here and there, but 20 years of dynamic balance are well ingrained.

> Doctors, nurses and other hospital staff are tripping on and ducking around a bird's nest of IV poles, fluid lines and electronic leads as I enter the operating room. There is not a glance in my direction. Karen is on the operating table. I know she is more scared than I. Baby's heart monitor is still stuttering, blinking on and off sporadically. The doctor is going to make his decision based on this. Delivering babies is not my area of expertise. However, I do know a thing or two about electrical instrumentation and an erratic signal that has a loose connection is unacceptable. In the climbing world we would call all this "a cluster fuck." I am standing by Karen's head and prancing like a father gorilla.

When I was ten, paramedics set my smashed tibia and fibula in a temporary splint before loading me into the ambulance. I had been hit by a car while riding my two-wheeler on the solid white centre-line of a two-way street. It was quite an event in our neighbourhood and all the kids lined up to sign or put their initials on my leg-length cast. It was not a week later that I tumbled while speeding around on my crutches. A follow up X-ray revealed that I had, indeed, knocked the bones out of alignment. A surgeon drilled seven holes into the shattered bones and installed a steel plate in order to fix them in place and give them a chance to mend.

In my early 30s the concept of "The Horizon of Social Acceptance" — the level of intensity on the curve between mania or introspection which most people can relate to — really gelled in my mind. If you cross The Horizon of Social Acceptance you are on your own. The unenlightened will describe exploits beyond it as either psycho, strange or dangerous. The exploits might be spiritual, such as hiding out with your computer for a long weekend and writing black poetry. Or they might be physical, like dangling 40 metres over the football field at McMahon Stadium in Calgary, Tyrolean traversing the two-inch steel cables that span high towers in each corner, solo, at night and in a snowstorm.

The year after I broke my leg I attempted an aerial traverse across our driveway on my hemp rope. I'd seen commandos in the movies hang from their hands, hook their legs over the rope and commando-crawl across a deep gorge. I strung my rope between the arms of two great maple trees, one on either side of our driveway about 20 feet up. Once I got the rope as tight as I could, I quickly began my commando-crawl. I was about halfway between the two trees when, without a hint of a warning, my rope snapped. I smacked the pavement with a clamorous crack. Rolling around in pain, I lay on the driveway with the wind knocked out of me. I hadn't got my breath when my neighbor showed up and standing over me, shook his head from side to side. He stared for a moment, then muttered, "You just never learn, do you Steve."

"Well," I thought, as I tossed my pack full of ice gear into the truck, "I wouldn't go that far."

Pounding tins of Ensure Plus and chugging Gatorade, I drove the miles to Yam. It looked clean and dry. In April of any year it was a definite gamble whether the face would have any snow on it. Walkman on, a few tins of Ensure in my pocket, I began the power hike up to the base. Groovin' to the tunes, I exhorted myself, "Surf the curve, man! Surf the curve! It's a mania day today, Stevie! Exploit exploit exploit!" I was also fully cognizant of the other extreme.

The climber who has the boldness to descend into the abyss in order that he may become more intimate with it — and with himself — and who has the power and discipline to arm his way back up the rope out of this darkness will grow spiritually at a rather alarming rate. Some of my most philosophical and emotional essays have been composed in this headspace. Once in a while, though, I would miscalculate and rap off of the end of the rope into a void of black poetry:

Ever try to have a conversation
While holding a gun to your own head?
Do you know how poignant every word can be
As it echoes down the barrel,
Or how futile.
Meaningless.
The trigger almost pulls itself.
Oh, the moments when I have the strength
To pull it away from my ear
And to channel such passion
Into something positive,
Or just into something.
For a moment breathing fully,
Feeling pain and joy
Simultaneously.
The Junkie.
Free for just a moment
From the shackle of this life.
Thank you, thank you.
But tomorrow is another day.
Yes, another fucking day.

I jam, stem and chimney up the first really technical and absurdly polished pitch on King's Chimney. There are, I am aware, situations in which one is bulldozed out of prolonged introspection.

The doctor looks at the blinking heart rate monitor still reading between 80 and 85. To me it looks like the front of a microwave oven bolted onto a cheap black box from Radio Shack. The handles on the light over the operating table appear to have Glad Baggies over them. This does not make sense to me. Somewhere out of my periphery water is running. I hear the snap of rubber gloves being stretched over chubby wrists.

"Let's go. It's going to be a section."

I stand ten feet tall and stare down at the doctor. We

make eye contact and I say, "Tell me. You are positive that is baby's heart rate?"

"Positive."

This pitch is always a bit gripping, awkward and bowling-alley smooth in spots. I really have to focus so a foot doesn't slip off. Pulling out of the slippery chimney, I recall with a bit of a chuckle how on one occasion I managed to kick-start a mania cycle from the depths of introspection.

As I strapped on my ice skates I tried to remember the last time I had been skating. Never having been a hockey player, I skated poorly at best. For this project, however, I really only needed to know how to stand up and go straight. It was around 10 p.m. and I was fully garbed in what I was later to call my "Urban Adventure Suit:" black insulated pants, black double-lined pile jacket, knee pads, elbow pads and home-made hip and tailbone pads (folded towels stuffed down my pants to protect bony protrusions), double-lined gloves and a cycling helmet. The last item, my ice-axe, was purely a precautionary measure. Any snow-and-ice man hurtling under the force of gravity will first attempt a self arrest using his ice-axe. I stood up on my ice skates, ice axe in hand, at the top of the bob sled track at Canada Olympic Park in Calgary.

"What's all the fuss about?" I had said as I walked beside the bobsled track earlier in the week. "This is a play-pen compared to even the easiest ice climbs." I was amazed at how low angle it was. "I could do this on ice skates!"

And so there I was. My skates cut parallel grooves in the ice as I accelerated more rapidly than I had anticipated. I crouched like a downhill ski racer, the serrated blade of my axe pick nicking the wall of the first corner as I tried to maintain balance. My "safety" device, I was discovering, was actually a liability in this endeavour. The jagged blade gouging the wall threatened to throw me off balance and send me into a cart-wheeling tumble. Going over the rail would be bad. This was keenly on my mind as my skates and legs started to get speed wobbles. Then I discovered that at top or "wobble" velocity I could crouch and sit on my tailbone pad. This checked my speed and brought my centre of gravity below the height of even the lowest sections of rail. All this I learned at 45 kilometres per hour.

Normally this section of the route is quite trivial. Today, however, the chimney is choked with unconsolidated snow. The grade increases to 5.7 or so, then to 5.8. As I bridge ever higher, another variable enters the equation: Verglas. I continue up the gully, the walls becoming ever smoother and the verglas more frequent. Before long I am suspended between chinks of rock poking through an armor of ice. The whole thing looks too much like a vertical luge track with fangs. A subtle snarl from this beast could send me over the rail.

Straining around the sinister armor of verglas, I downclimb the rock, craving the sharp, serrated blade of my ice axe. Hanging there, as if frozen in a still frame, I have the luxury that most bobsledders don't: To study the adversity while in it, to avoid a catastrophic over-the-rail wreck. I decide to inch out left and see if I can traverse into a different pitch at mid-height. I postulate that if I can make it out left, I would prefer to on-sight solo a dry 5.5 pitch than deal with the latticework of the luge track directly above. I shut my Walkman off. Time to focus.

A white sheet is strung up at Karen's midsection. There is a clatter of stainless steel surgical tools jostling on a metal tray. I hold Karen's hand. She is fully conscious. A nurse paints iodine on Karen's abdomen with a broad brown brush. The smell makes my nostrils quiver. I start to sweat. The sheet fogs into a white blur as I begin to experience a new type of risk. A different kind of concern, a further form of fear. All very primal. Our child, my offspring, my wife: All potentially in peril. I am aware of my excited state and the fact that I must flatline right now. Karen needs me.

In times of extreme mania there can be a tendency to lose focus and waste valuable energy. We often experience the perils of high excitation through fear. We lose motor control. Our joints stiffen. Our physical and mental capabilities plummet. In these situations, one must enter yet another altered state I call "Manic Meditation," where we maintain that high level of energy and intensity but with control and precision. Flatlining while in a heightened state of mania.

I am cognisant of this paradigm as I begin an uncertain traverse towards this route to the left. The first few moves around the arête are tricky. I have to be sure I can reverse them. If I get stuck midway across this traverse, unable to continue either up or down, there will be no one to pluck me off and carry me back to the ground. My rap line, I am also aware, is 2,000 feet below in the truck. I climb out of the relative security of the playpen and into an expansive grey mist of limestone. It looks blank. My spine tingles as I take a deep, even breath.

We all surf our own curves. Some of us need more risk before we have to kick into Manic Meditation. I have often joked, while drinking my fifth cup of coffee, that I am a "low idler" and that I am not truly awake unless I am risking my life.

"Okay, OK," I whisper to myself, "I'm awake." Focusing through this mist of stone, I scan the rock for about 45 seconds until I distinguish a dark circular shape. It is the eye of a piton poking out of a tight seam. Under further scrutiny, holds seem to take form out of this fog in the direction of the pin. The piton, I am acutely aware, may not be on the pitch. It might be an old rap anchor. My instinct says, "go have a look." Three digits on one hand sink into a wonderfully prickly jug. My other hand is massaged by a surface of baby shark's teeth on another hold. It's sticky rubber sashays on some smears. The holds continue to come and soon I can see station anchors. I'm rockin' up the crag again. Rippin' down the scree on the backside of Yam I am mindful that …

Generally, in the hush of deep introspection the allure of the "impossible" or "just possible" seems more powerful. The rush becomes problem solving through such improbable endeavours using skill, experience and psycho/physical prowess. At other times, tribulation is completely beyond your control.

My ears are straining for our baby's first cry. A doctor and two nurses work with fervor. I'm gripped. So gripped, that I stay low behind the white sheet. So low, that all I can see is the surgeon's jaw muscle glistening and twitching behind his mask. I'm not a blood guy. Need to flatline. Don't want to pass out.

I reach the Yam parking lot. It's just before 2:00 p.m. After changing my socks, I strap on my roller blades, quaff a few more tins of Ensure Plus, throw three more into a fanny pack, chug a litre of Gatorade and begin the 50-mile rollerblade back to Calgary.

The road is rough. I can feel the vibration through my skates, up my shins and in my knees. After three hours, I sit on a guard-rail at the side of the road, take off my blades, and push the soles of my feet into coarse gravel trying to massage away the pain of pressure points. The cold pebbles feel good on the hot spots. Cars zoom past as the sharp steel plate of the guard-rail begins to cut into my buttocks.

For the first time all day I feel alone and lonely. The wind and the rough road have slowed my progress, almost doubled my estimated time on this leg. I have not brought enough food, and food is fuel. The fact that I have under dressed for the wind further leaks away my fuel reserves. By my estimate, my carbohydrate reserves will run out just about now. I curse myself. These are avoidable mistakes solely due to my miscalculation. The game transforms and now it is to keep my heart rate low enough to allow my body to metabolize fat into clean-burning fuel. I am mindful that it is only a stopgap manoeuvre.

I put my skates back on and begin again my methodical strides. If I allow my heart rate to get too high my body will start filling the fuel void by burning blood sugar. A blood sugar crash now, after 11 hours of effort, would finish me. Again, a tightrope: Blading in balance between speed and physiological fuel constraints. I enter an "Enduro-Trance," a kind of meditation that focuses on efficiency of movement and progress, rather than on pain and self-pity.

I re-ask myself the age old question: Is it more difficult to handle a situation where you can't just quit? Like this morning on the ice and rock, where quitting means death. Or is it more challenging to continue when quitting is simple? Like right now. I could just stop, stand right here and hitch a ride.

It's too late when I realize that I've gone too hard. The delicate balance is blown and I falter on the tightrope. Swooning on my blades, the last remaining calories of blood sugar spark, sputter and fizzle. The void is deep. I stumble and catch myself with the crook of my elbow on the taut line. My feet dangle in the wind. I fail at a scissor kick in an attempt to hook a knee over the wire in commando- crawl fashion. If only I had a carabiner I could clip. My fingers begin to open on the cold steel cable. Both hands fail simultaneously and I plummet, then crater in a blood sugar crash. As I stagger into a gas station, the girl's eyes widen behind the counter as she asks, "Are you having fun roller blading?" My silence turns the heads of the other customers.

There is little chatter in the operating room. To me, the quiet is greater than the acres of vertical limestone in the Bow Valley as I listen for protracted minutes for the cry that means the life and living of our child. I can only hear the doctor and nurse's sterile gowns chafing against each other as they huddle over Karen and fervently but precisely cut through the wall of her stomach. A splash of red spatters his white sterile mask. I cannot watch. I never wanted to hear a baby cry more in my life.

Perhaps the most problematic situation of all is when the relative amplitudes of mania and introspection max out and the frequency approaches infinity. What does this mean? You are swinging, well beyond the Horizon of Social Acceptance, from extreme mania to severe introspection so rapidly that for all practical purposes you are simultaneously in introspection and mania at acute levels. You need to storm a mountain and recite your blackest poetry all at the same time. I call this "The Zone." In this purgatory impossible odds may entice, because failure is seen as punishment for mediocrity. Amidst The Zone's trickery, however, there is also a possibility that your whole being may rise up in revolt of facing certain failure with an off-the-charts intensity.

Standing at the bar, minding my own business, I notice a peanut shell falling like a small piece of ice into the crook of my elbow. I give it a wiggle and it slips easily away onto the plank wood floor. I don't see the avalanche coming. It bludgeons down the slope and blasts me like a battering ram. I have entered The Zone.

A sweat breaks above my hairline and creeps around my ears. Large beads trickle down my jaw and dangle off my chin, freezing into sharp icicles. These snap off and make a pile of ice shards on the floor. All conversation turns to noise. The people around me wear headlamps which only further illuminates my desperation. The air becomes thick with ice crystals that are smothering. In this cart-wheeling tumble I clench my ice axe and manage to make my way out the door to hail a cab like a rescue chopper. Outside are two big cowboys wearing trench coats. They challenge me to a fight. My biceps begin to twitch and I struggle to speak clearly, "It appears to me that you guys just stepped over the rail of your playpen." The claws of The Zone have me fully in a stranglehold and I continue to hiss, "All guarantees of your physical safety have vaporized." There is a flurry of ice axes, cowboy hats, avalanche dust, trench coats and peanut shells. A policeman digs me out of the avalanche debris. Two cowboys lie sprawled on top of the snow.

Before squaring off against the crux of the roller blading leg, a mile and then some up the Cochrane Hill, I rummage around in the road gutter and find a large piece of cardboard and a plastic bag both covered with road salt. I stuff the cardboard down my shirt for insulation and to help cut the wind. The plastic bag I tie around my head for a hat. Just after 9:00 p.m. I am hurtling down a steep hill on Nose Hill Drive in Calgary. I've been going for 14 hours and discover, too late, that I've misjudged the turn onto my street. The curb approaches my blades at 40 kilometres per hour. Dial in Stevie! This is it!

My wheels ricochet off the curb like a staccato of machine gun fire. I hurl through the air, tuck, hit the ground, and like a 190 pound Nadia Comeneci, instinctively do a shoulder roll and stand up on my skates still doing 30 kilometres per hour. I chortle to myself "I've still got it!" By 10:00 p.m. I am on my bicycle heading back to Yam to pick up the truck. I have no spare tube or patch kit. This is yet one more very careless oversight.

And where does the ego fit in the paradigm of mania, introspection and risk taking? "The Ego Drive" can move one into grand exploits, "The Ego Dive" can send one into hiding for weeks. I have gone and soloed rock climbs to give myself a bit of a kick in the self-esteem department. I have also turned downclimbing exploits in moments of deep introspection, recognizing I was just not up to such challenges.

I become gripped about getting a flat tire. In and of itself a flat tire is not necessarily gripping. At this point, however, I am trashed and riding the ragged edge. I have not fully recovered from my blood sugar crash. I could ride on the flat or walk with the bike if I had to. By now I am imprisoned by my vision. Escape will come only through completion. I will do whatever it takes to get my bicycle across the finish line. And yes, my ego is involved.

> Finally I hear the loud squeal. Simultaneously the doctor announces, "It's a girl!" Air touches her lungs for the first time. I glance over the curtain carefully and see her squirm lively in the doctors hands. "She's beautiful." Karen and I share tears. I nuzzle her as she lies there and the doctor and nurses make the first inspection of our little girl.

A spasm in my neck encourages me to sit up and ride with no hands when the road is flat to ease this pain. I have not been hunched over on my road bike all winter and curiously my neck hurts more than any other part of my body. The Gatorade in my water bottle freezes and I dehydrate further. The full moon makes my headlamp mostly unnecessary, though I turn it on for a particularly rough section of road. The beam forms a white circle of light around my front wheel like a stippled canvas sheet with a black border. The road steepens. Hair bristles on my scalp as I become aware of the long harsh pedal strokes I continue to paint onto this coarse cloth. The outer border of this rutted fabric remains just beyond my reach, provisionally paralyzing me in purgatory.

To a degree, we all measure our self worth against our endeavours and exploits. When mania is aligned with socially acceptable behaviors society rewards us: We are creative, an artist, an innovator or a genius. The same applies for introspection. On the other hand, when the extremes of mania or introspection manifest themselves in venues on the dark side, we are shunned, disrespected and in some cases "put away."

Karen is wheeled into the recovery room. She is drained. The last 35 hours have ground her down. The drugs have fully taken and she falls into an exhausted and drug-induced sleep. The midwife has baby Stephanie in one hand and Karen's breast in the other. Stephanie latches on and eats her first food.

Swerving to avoid a pothole, I am again 10 years old, riding on the solid white centre-line. Seven screw holes shiver even though they are now sated with bone. My shin tingles as I shoulder-check and speedily steer back to the roadside. The outline of my truck finally comes into view as a dark shape beside the road. Gravel grunts under my skinny tires as I ride up and dismount. The rear window of my truck is broken. Filled with a sudden uneasiness, I stand there on the broken glass. My headlamp further illuminates the dread: My rock and ice gear have been stolen. I climb in behind the wheel, start the engine and turn on the headlights. The reality of this financial avalanche assaults me as I hang frantically onto the faded hemp rope of my success. In the bright light I can no longer see the stars and the moonlight dims. I stare into the white pool the headlights make on the gravel. Again, my whole periphery is overwhelmed with a wall of white. This time, though, blackness invades like the closing aperture in a camera until only a pinhole of light remains. I become mindful that the realization of my sculpture is complete as this last glimmer fades to black.

"Hold Stephanie's head like this, and Karen's breast this way. This is a good latch."

The midwife coaches me for two or three minutes, is obviously satisfied and leaves without a word. The stretcher is quite high and is very awkward. After a few minutes my neck starts to hurt and my arms are cramping. I glance around the room for help. There is none. I am it. Our 53 minute-old baby is solely reliant on me. As the crick in my neck spasms down my back, I become aware that what I am doing is a very true definition of responsibility.

I'm sitting in my corner office shuffling paper and sipping my fifth cup of coffee. Cutting my finger while removing a staple, I stare at the blood running down my hand and then laugh to myself. I am about as far away from hand jams, cauliflower heads and bob-sled tracks as one can get. Things have been relatively quiet on the Mania/Introspection front — nowhere even close to beyond The Horizon of Social Acceptance. Stephanie is three months old. We have just bought her a Fold&Go playpen. I have begun to recog-nise that Surfin' the Curve at will is actually a tremendous luxury that I have had for most of my life. Stephanie brings us great joy, but how will she and our future children fit into the model? Will she be a dampening factor which will limit my exploits, manic or introspective, in the physical and intellectual arenas that are well beyond The Horizon of Social Acceptance? What about ego? Will gymnastic and mental restraint over greater periods of time in-still enhanced amplitudes beyond which I have yet experienced? I don't know.

Holding a tissue to my finger, being careful not to get blood on my starched white shirt, I walk over to my window and stare down 300 feet into the street below. Glancing out over north Calgary, I notice a large black bird soaring in updrafts made by the Chinook wind. It is the raven. He dives headfirst into a spiralling plummet and seems out of control for several seconds. Quickly though, he ar-rests his plunge and again hovers in the updraft as if to caw, "And what about risk?"

It's a good question. And one that has been much on my mind. I have yet to experience and then reflect on this new sensitivity. I turn and stare through the inner glass wall of my office and see my boss, our department vice-president, at the end of the hall. I turn back and face the raven.

"I did just recently execute a high risk and very politically sensi-tive decision here at the office. Most of my colleagues, including my boss, disagreed with my process of implementation. I paraphrase their comments: 'You will put yourself out of a job,' 'It's political suicide,' 'It's your power you are eroding,' 'It's a blasphemy,' 'This will mean the end of your department,' 'Is this the beginning of the end of your group?' 'You do that and we are finished!'"

The issue had obsessed me, waking me up nights, distracting me while cuddling Stephanie, instilling twinges of stomach pain, trashing me to such an extent mentally that I had little energy left for physical exercise. In the execution of the endeavour I was alone. Was this naïve? Stupid? Brilliant? Time will tell.

Once again I suddenly become vigilant. I am beyond The Horizon of Social Acceptance, commando-crawling across a tightrope, my old hemp chord held in tension between the arms of power and politics, balanced and judged, I hope, by the value added to the shareholder.

The raven's black eyes seem to connect with mine in understanding. In the tinted glass I see my reflection. My left hand removes the tissue from my right hand and squeezes the end of my finger. A bubble of blood forms, its surface under tension. I hold it up to my eyes and watch it balloon. Then my eyes focus on the reflection of my white dress shirt in the window. The white expands into a broad canvas. I curl my lip in an intense grin as my finger paints a harsh stroke of blood across my shirt. I chortle loud enough that the raven and my secretary hear my cackle. "SURF THE CURVE MAN! SURF THE CURVE!"

# 2001 & Beyond

My new world involves a second child Joseph and measuring risk versus reward in the financial arena on a daily basis. A new brand of stakeholder is considered in my risk/reward continuum — the shareholder. Is my cup full?

Amongst all this, I have a hankering for the north-west wall of Windtower and get in over my head. All this is juxtaposed against my first experiences on Windtower during "The Hard Years."

# Windtower: A Journey Revisited

My brain is tricked by the optical illusion created by several planes of overhanging rock above me. The slope that falls away below this north face further complicates the optics. Subsequently, when I let go of the etrier, I am surprised to find that I accelerate in a long swing to the right. The lip of a large overhang grates the rope like a giant saw as I pendulum further and further to the right. I am 80 feet off the tarmac. If the rope cuts through I will die. My only thought is, "Jesus Christ, I'm a dad! I'm a dad!"

At the same instant I throw my hand in between the rock and the rope, attempting to keep the rope off the sharp edge. Feverishly, I try to get some leverage on it. My feet, however, only churn uselessly in space. It is impossible to create a gap between the rope, my hand and the rock. My palm grips the rope, protecting it. The back of my hand lacerates along the lip of the overhang. My list of possible options is short and poor: Remove my hand from the veritable saw blade and risk cutting the rope clean through, or leave it carving along the rock, mincing the skin and possibly the tendons on the back of my hand. I decide on the latter, yet continue to make feeble attempts to keep the back of my hand off the serrated edge. Finally my swing slows and stops. The rope is intact. The skin on the back of my hand looks like it has been buckshot. Ridges of skin stick out like tufts of pilling pile. Before I feel pain I feel stupid.

As blood begins to drip off my hand and I wait for the pounding in my head to abate, I stare for a moment into the Bow Valley below. My god! Five thousand days and nights ago I was here. How many hours had I spent looking out at this view while Jeff Marshall and I had toiled on countless attempts over the summers of 1986, '87 and '88 on this face? After being stormed off on our first attempt in 1986, we had ventured into the Rose and Crown in Canmore and reported, "We are definitely not putting up a classic." It turned out to be more difficult than either of us had ever experienced. In our toil we had gained an intimate respect for the delicate nature of the limestone medium and the necessity of a tight-knit partnership. We had talked little about risk and rarely about reward. However, we had shared a common need, a need to cut the edge of our potential; to experience, if only for a moment, the true outer limits of our psycho-physical abilities. The result had been Iron Butterfly, 5.11, A4.

While climbing Iron Butterfly I had studied another line off to the right: A tight steep corner with a big crack in the back. This line would share the same first pitch, then follow a series of ledges into the main corner system. In the years that followed, this "other" route on Windtower was never far from my conscious mind.

How many times had I retired from serious climbing since 1988? Several times. I had been essentially a recreational climber between 1990 and '97. My mountains were completing my engineering and MBA degrees during those years. I did, though, climb somewhat seriously in '97/'98. In '97 I got fired up and returned to free East End Boys, a project that had been much on my mind since Bill Betts and I had completed the first ascent. After that season I decided to focus on my career, got married and had our first child, Stephanie. I quit my job in October of 2000, put a group of investors together and started a resource company: Efficient Energy Resources Ltd.

This corporate endeavour was a significant challenge, but by April 2001 I was having climbing pangs. Clearly I had not settled into the cauldron of new life experiences and responsibilities. In my other life, Windtower had been a place of comfortable discomfort, intense passion and learning, a fight of fights, where Jeff Marshall and I had slashed our cocoons with daggers and emerged as "Iron Butterflies," tough, yet with a delicate touch, to tap and pat our way up the formidable and overhanging northwest face — a limestone flower to which we returned many times over the three year period to drink its nectar. Thirteen years later, now a tarnished, bent and dented insect, I wanted to drink again from this flower. Selfish? Noooo. Just because I now had a wife and child, and had just started a company with investors who stood to lose a lot of money if I got killed, was to me not worth a second thought. And anyway, as a rock climb how dangerous could it be? Besides, I had already climbed the face once, so really it would not be any overwhelming risk that I would be taking.

So it began, like an old warhorse smelling again the traces of smoke and gunpowder floating on the breeze from the front and hearing the cannons just over the horizon. It made me bristle with excitement. I began to strain on the bridle of my farming tackle. I glanced behind me to see only the blade of my plough carving a neat swath in the brown soil. A tidy farmhouse and barn were the full focus of my world. It was with a very small flame of enthusiasm and with quite low expectations that I began to take small steps towards preparing again for the battlefield. There was, in fact, very little discretionary time for climbing between dadhood, spousehood and career commitments. Only one day a weekend and one evening during the week. Needless to say, by the time July rolled around, the old warhorse was not ready for the fight that was coming.

During my last exodus from retirement I had done some climbing with Raphael Slawinski. He was an exceptional gentlemen as well as a star climber. In 2001 I had also cold-called Eric Dumerac and suggested we do a route together. Eric too, was a "superclimber with a passion for first ascents." As Urs Kallen used to say, "If you want to climb hard routes, climb with good guys!" I began planting seeds with these two for a one-push attempt at this new line. It became obvious very quickly that I would be the weak link on this team.

By virtue of all my previous visits to the wall, we were well informed as to what was in store for us. Before my first attempt with Jeff Marshall in 1986 the only information we had on the face came from the 1970s when some of the old guard had gone up for a look. They soon scurried away when an aged winter cornice, falling from the upper reaches of the face, landed 60 feet out from the base of the wall.

It was May 1986. I had just driven 2000 miles from Ontario and had been in Calgary only eight hours. My first stop was the MEC (Mountain Equipment Coop). When inquiring about routes on Yam, I was ushered over to a short guy with a ponytail behind the climbing counter. "Oh great," I thought, "another one of these arrogant pony-tailed climbing store super-heroes." I again asked about routes on Yam.

"What grade do you climb?"

Here we go. "5.9, 5.10." I replied, shaving a full grade off what I knew I could on-sight on new ground.

"Well, this is limestone around here and you'll have to shave a grade or two off of that."

Of course I'd grown up on the limestone of the Niagara Escarpment in Southern Ontario. And though the cliffs were only 80 to 150 feet high, we had a strict ground up ethic for completing first ascents and never pre-rehearsed routes. It was on-sight lead and clean as you climb, throwing loose rock off as you went. I didn't know it at the time, but this was the perfect training ground for doing first ascents on the limestone faces in the Rockies.

Jeff walked me through several of the 5.7 and 5.8 routes on Yam and then I asked him if he knew where there were any parks in Calgary.

"Parks?"

"Yeah parks. You know, like where kids play and there are trees and stuff."

I could see he was puzzled. "Uh yeah, there are parks … Why do you ask?"

"I want to set up my Bachar ladder so I can train."

It was then that Jeff got an understanding look in his eye. Our spirits connected and he said, "Hey, what are you doing later? I'm heading out to the Big Rock to go bouldering after work. Would you like to come?" And that was the beginning of our partnership. We were new-routing on Yam within weeks.

Only a few days later, during one of my sojourns between Calgary, Yam and Canmore, the car swerved left, and then right as my head, like a pinball in a pinball machine, went from one side of my '74 Nova to the other as my eyes attempted to take in all the expanses of unclimbed rock in the Bow Corridor. Suddenly I screeched the Nova onto the shoulder. I was out of the car hyperventilating with excitement, staring up at the northwest face of Windtower while my antiquated hunk of iron made its final groan, blowing black smoke out at me from under the hood. The mountain beckoned me, seducing me to submit to its great wall that loomed dark above me. I stood there, visualizing the moment when I would hang from its steep cracks and struggle to find purchase in its acres of incipient seams. I wanted to extend my physical and psychological limits by day and drink in the acrid air that is so close to a limestone wall on a still night; to revere in the light of a new day and in the pleasure that comes from scored and bleeding hands that work to haul the bags up yet another pitch. This I knew would be a new personal frontier.

The next time I spoke to Jeff, I asked him about the face. As fate and fortune would have it, he had had a crush on the face since he was a kid. The game was set. We would climb the face in a single three-day push over the July long weekend of 1986.

It is not a difficult task to convince Eric and Rafael to attempt the "other" line on the face. Windtower is a beautiful mountain. It looks a lot like Dracula's castle with ramparts and twin summits. The northwest face still has seen only one ascent. It would be gratifying to push another line up the wall, to complete the second ascent of the face via a new route. All this is my pitch to Raphael and Eric. The weather is perfect. Too perfect. I feel I need a north wall warm up and suggest finishing a route on The Ship's Prow near Canmore as a training climb. Secretly, I know I need a warm up — I have not been on new ground since our daughter Stephanie was born. I also am not sure how my head is going to fare in this new paradigm of "dadhood." And then I, the one pitching, get pitched. "We should do the bigger route first. This weather can't last." I had got the train rolling and now it is to be unstoppable. I am unable to argue with the logic, so I concur and bury my trepidation. Secretly though, I am quite gripped about the whole affair.

In June of 1986 there was a new routing storm on Yamnuska. I'd tagged along on the first ascent of Astro Yam with Jeff and Brian Gross, made the first ascent of East End Boys with Bill Betts and completed the solo first ascent of Highlander, as well as the second free ascent of CMC Wall. Jeff and I were feeling confident and planned our venture onto Windtower. We had our standard rack: Full set of friends (in those days that was only sizes 1 through 4, with half sizes), a selection of 10 pitons and perhaps 10 bolts, along with 10 or 12 quick draws on long slings. We had hammocks, etriers and jumars.

The long weekend in July came and Jeff and I hiked up the drainage, over the Windtower-Rimwall col and up to the base of the wall. We knew roughly where we wanted to go but the features would decide exactly. In 300 feet of wall along the base of the face, there was really only one place with reasonable access onto the upper wall. There was a large over hang about 80 feet up, just off to the right. There was a weakness just to the left off this overhang. Jeff and I scrambled up perhaps 60 feet to a point where the climbing got difficult. It was my lead.

The old warhorse has not carried a load this heavy for several years. Farming has made him soft. The load of the cannon and the hauling tackle chaff the horse's neck and shoulders. The calloused tissue necessary for such labour has long gone. His shod feet hurt on the sharp stones. The short distance to the front nearly spends him.

I am probably an hour behind Eric and Rafael by the time I reach the base of the route. It is eerie being back here. I stare at features that I had last looked at in June of 1988. My God! I was still that naïve passionate climber then. Two months later, in '88, Brian Wallace had been killed on our attempt to complete the first ascent of the north face of Mount Lougheed. A lot has changed since then ...

> At the base of the first pitch, about 60 feet up a fourth class scramble, Jeff and I did not put a belay in. I would try to get something in as soon as I could. The wall steepened up quickly and the climbing got tough right away. There would not be any good gear for as far as my eyes could see. I managed, balancing on a sloping ledge, to drill the first bolt on the pitch, the first bolt on the route, and the first protection between Jeff and myself. The limestone was harder than that of Yamnuska and it took about twice as long to drill a bolt.

Rafael will take the first pitch this time. It is clear to me that there is no way in hell that I am going to lead it. It had been a memorable lead 15 years before when I had been at the top of my game. We, too, do not put a belay in. Raf ties into the sharp end and starts up the pitch. It gets hard right away. I have acute confidence in Rafael's ability, but cannot help but look at the scree 60 feet below. If a hold breaks, tied together we'd both deck out.

"Ummm — Eric? Would you mind terribly tying on my hammer and a few pins? I want to put a belay in here."

Raf glances over his shoulder, a bit fussed about the sudden delay that I have thrown into the start of his lead. I whack two good pins in. Once clipped, I feel much better.

> Above the bolt I managed to sneak a few stoppers in that were only OK. This was a "no fall situation." If I fell from high above my gear, these pieces would all rip out and I would hit the ramp below the first bolt. My tib, fib and femur would be crushed or snapped as they tried to absorb the energy of the fall before the rope came tight. This was not a good place to fall. I was full of confidence, however, and powered up the next section. I was run out about 20

feet on overhanging terrain when I realized I had hit a dead end. I glanced over to my right and could see a line of holds going through the bulge and up to a small stance. They were about eight feet to my right. Nonetheless, I could not get there from here. A solid pump developed in my forearms. I began breathing deeply and made a loud blowing sound through my lips as I exhaled.

At some time in my formative years I had developed a habit of breathing this way when I was run out, pumped and needed to concentrate. The sound was somewhat akin to that of an old steam train. Jeff maintained that he always gripped the rope tighter when I began breathing that way.

*The wings of the Iron Butterfly strain against the straight jacket of the cocoon. The confines of the heavy cloth insulate it from the dangers of the outside world. Protect it even, from itself, until its development is complete and it is able to survive in the merciless outside world. This is the way of nature. With gritted teeth, it hisses, "I'm ready! I'm ready! I'm ready!"*

"Okay Stevie, this is why you practice down-climbing."
So I downclimbed the bulge, made a tricky traverse right to the line of holds and then re-climbed through the bulge to the small stance.

It is interesting that today's novices learning to sport climb are taught merely to jump off when they are pumped or have climbed a sequence incorrectly. No instruction is given on where to fall and where not to fall. Many of these novices or intermediate climbers implement this same tactic in no fall situations, often with ankle-breaking consequences.

I was pumped and breathing heavily when I arrived at two small footholds where I could stand in balance under a small overlap and get a bit of a rest. I was fit and knew I would recover within a few minutes. I placed some more small wires on my way up another 30 feet to another set of biggish footholds. Then I managed to tap in a knife-blade piton. This gave me a brief respite, albeit only a psychological one, as I scoped the wall above. It was clear the gymnastic difficulties were not over. I placed another bolt.

At this point I was about half a rope length up, at the height of the eight-foot roof just off to my right. I had one quick-draw left, having placed a lot of body-weight wires in the first 80 feet. Like I always say: "If you don't put it in, it definitely won't hold." I did not want to set a station here, so I lowered off and back-cleaned all of the body-weight pieces and then elevatored back up to my high point, replenished with my climbing toys. This placing of body-weight pieces on free climbing pitches was a tactic that I had developed while climbing on the Niagara Escarpment. By placing gear that could hold a slip (but not much more), you could string together an otherwise virtually protectionless pitch with some degree of safety. Of course, there would be moments where you were virtually soloing, but a body-weight placement would give you a five-foot section of rock as a small sanctuary. I also theorized that if five pieces pulled, they would absorb some energy and could help slow down a fall enough so that the sixth piece might actually hold. In this case, once I had got some bombproof protection in, I lowered off and took the laundry off the line so to speak.

Raf is perhaps the strongest traditional limestone climber in Canada. He has climbed virtually all of the routes of any significance, freed many of the routes put up by Jeff and myself and put up several of his own. He has started repeating routes that 15 years ago were considered death routes because he has climbed everything else! Still, I consider this pitch one of my best on-sights on new ground and quite a serious lead, so I give him as much beta as I can.

Eric is still busy packing up the gear down and to the right. He is a keen and talented climber, known in particular for his desperate and visionary mixed climbs, who takes great pride in setting his routes up for others to enjoy. He has a keen sense of humour and a compassionate side that is seldom seen in climbers of his calibre.

As Jeff cleaned the pitch, I told him to remove the bolt hangers — "they cost $3.00 you know." Jeff removed both the hanger and the cap screw. I had actually meant that he leave the cap screw so that future parties could at least have something to put a wired stopper over to provide some security.

I realized, even at the time, that it would be tough for future parties to bring the correct size cap-screw with the exact thread size up on the wall and then have to re-place it along with the hanger. Later I was to be cursed for removing bolt hangers by climbers repeating my routes. Curiously, the view 15 years later, when it became the norm to build routes with future ascents in mind, was that there was some bizarre, malicious intent behind this practice. They were reading way too much into it. I was living on about $6,000 a year at the time and climbing lots. A $3.00 hanger was one less beer I could have. Also, it never occurred to us to consider future parties. Looking back, anything was fair game: If there were six rap slings on a rap anchor and five looked good enough and the sixth was brand new, I would take the sixth and add it to my rack. Or if downclimbing looked possible, I'd remove the whole anchor as booty. Less frequently, I would climb the most travelled routes and if a piton was placed beside a good stopper or friend crack, I'd remove the piton and add it to my rack as well. This was not an ethical statement of any kind whatsoever, it was merely what I called "booty patrol." Of course, finding a route that someone had rapped off from five or six pitches up and subsequently removing all of the gear from their rap stations, was considered a tremendous find.

As Rafael started up the pitch he could not even find the bolthole in which to place a cap-screw with a new hangar. So similar to what I had done, he stood in precarious balance on the sloping ledge and placed a new bolt and continued up the pitch.

*The Iron Butterfly fashions a crude but sharp knife from iron fillings embedded in the fabric of the cocoon. It begins slowly but methodically sawing through the cotton-canvass-like cloth that binds it.*

> The next section was steep and looked hard and tough to protect. The wall was overhanging below. I chortled, "Yuh uh uh!" I could go for it here. I had good toys in. If I blew off it would be all airtime and the rope would absorb the energy of the fall. Not my tib, fib and femur. This, was a place to fall.

Back in my formative years while doing first ascents ground up on the Niagara Escarpment, I had often found myself in similar situations. In many places the escarpment is capped by dolomite, a harder rock than the limestone underneath and typically less fractured. Usually it offers fewer opportunities for protection, if any. (We did not drill bolts in those days, it being considered bad style and unethical by most climbers in Southern Ontario.)

At the junction of the two rock types there were often substantial overhangs. On many occasions I found myself standing at a small stance underneath these overhangs 80 feet off the deck, contemplating launching into no-man's land above where I would likely have to run it out 30 or 40 feet with no protection. Usually the wall overhung below, so if the anchors held these were actually relatively safe places from which to fall. I developed the habit of placing five or six anchors at or just below the dolomite cap and then charging above with full confidence. When I was 25 feet out I did not want to be second-guessing the quality of my protection. I knew from experience that this would cause me to freeze up and fall off for sure. In rock geometries, where the wall overhung below and there was clearly little or no protection above, I used to say, "put in a belay — clip all the anchors into the rope — and go for it!" Often I made it in one go up these blank headwalls. I also took several 80-foot screamers. On one memorable occasion I powered out five feet from easy ground and was facing a 70-foot fall. I simply could not hang on any longer. I knew, again from experience, that it was better to fall off in control than to blow off in a slip half-way through a gymnastic move. Two moments before I would have fallen off anyway, I yelled down to my belayer, "Coming off man! Take it in! Take it right fucking in! Pull me off!" With all that rope out, I wanted to remove as much slack out of the system as possible before I stepped off the cliff. In that moment it was comforting to feel the pull of the rope downwards on my harness knowing that I had reduced my fall distance by perhaps five feet. This few pounds of extra force on my fingertips finished me and I stepped out and away from the rock. Gravity took care of the rest. My belayer and friend said afterward, "That was the farthest fall I have ever seen! It was amazing! The rope came down, sliding through all the runners, stacking itself on the ledge and then, like a shot, quickly disappeared!"

This was akin to a "dolomite cap" situation. I chalked up. Then I chalked up again. This time I began my breathing before I left the stance. There was a short traverse to the right, then I had to launch up another steep groove. The holds came and went. Twenty-five feet higher I found some protection and was soon padding up steep corners. The pro was adequate. I had some good pieces, but many were bodyweight placements. Having again used up all the gear on the rack, I clipped my chalk bag into the last wire before a good-sized ledge. I had two carabiners and the bolt kit left on the rack. I drilled two bolts and brought Jeff up. When he reached the belay he commented, "That is the most impressive lead on rock I have ever seen." I was grateful for the compliment.

*With one final cut, the Butterfly's wings burst through the slice made in the cocoon, like a kid's pop-up toy, tearing the hole larger in the process. As it stretches its limbs, the insect feels currents of air on its wings for the first time.*

I palmed and smeared my way up the steep corner on pitch 3. I was intrigued by the difference of the rock texture here when compared with that of Yamnuska. On Windtower there were vast expanses of smooth and almost featureless rock. It was less busted up as well, the cracks tending to be tighter, more like seams. And then I looked up. I guess it made sense; this was a north wall and overhanging. This part of the face did not see any sunlight, so the freeze thaw action was minimal.

I stemmed across a shallow corner and placed the tip of a knife-blade into a crack. Retrieving my hammer from my holster, I gave the blade a couple of good taps. At around knee height I noticed two very small pebbles fall out of the bottom of the crack. I felt a tingling in my chest that I knew to be shots of adrenalin. They did not create fear, nor cause me to lose motor control. They sharpened my senses, making me acutely aware of even the smallest details. They also made me focus. Somehow these situations must have burned deep neuronic pathways in my brain, because my recall of many of these incidents is acute, even 17 years later.

Leaving the piton in, I climbed back down one move and then tapped the rock just below the pin. A hollow "bum-mm bummm bummm" reverberated from behind a flake about seven feet long and three feet across! Above it was extremely difficult ground that would need to be climbed on direct aid. So the transition between free climbing and aid was right at this flake. There were no edges to hook or other seams to the right or left of the flake that I could use to get past it. The only weakness was the fracture behind the flake itself.

I decided to drill two bolts one above the other on the right side of the flake. The second would get me high enough to be able to lever the flake off while at the same time stay out of its way when it went. I clipped both ropes into each bolt, then lowered off and took out all of my anchors back to the belay about 60 feet down and to my left. Jeff would have slight protection from a direct hit by virtue of the geometry of the wall and the fact that he was out to the left.

"Okay man. Elevator going up!"

I hauled myself back up by pulling on the dead line as Jeff took in the slack. When I arrived back at the bolts and stared back down the wall, it occurred to me that even though I had cleared the ropes as best I could, there was still potential for this huge flake to chop the ropes on the way down as it fell. Hmmm ... We climbed on double ropes so what were the chances? I decided to hard-clip my two bolts with a sling for the trundling process.

The tip of the pick on my rock hammer fitted neatly into a slot in the crack about a third of the way down from the top of the flake. With one hand on my hammer and the other holding the ropes up and away from the rock, I managed to create a bit of a catenary curve in the ropes away from the wall and down to the left.

"Okay man! Here it comes!"

I saw Jeff's red helmet disappear from view. Using my hammer like a crowbar, I cranked on the flake. It moved half an inch. Bits of gravel began trickling out of the bottom of the crack below me. I gave another yank. The flake leaned out from the wall like a sentry struck by an archer's arrow, frozen against gravity, momentarily stalled before teetering beyond the point of no return. Its plummet began with a groan of rock on rock. Then came the tinkle of pebbles dropping, freed from their long stay wedged between the main wall and the flake. There was silence for an instant. Then came a roar like cannons firing upon us as the flake hit the ramp below and exploded into 5000 pieces. The sheer violence of it vibrated our entire bodies. And then, finally, the sulphurous smell of blasted rock filled our nostrils.

The ropes, thankfully, were intact.

"James? You OK down there?"

A red helmet re-appeared. "Yeah. That was a big one."

*The Butterfly, startled and frightened by the roar, hovers momentarily in the dust-filled air, but soon lands back on the flower. After all, this is what it had dreamed about.*

While jumaring I examine every rock feature with intrigue. I find my old bolt hole down and slightly left of where Raf drilled the new bolt. It is rusty and looks old. I would have drilled a new one too. I carry on removing Raf's gear. Eventually I arrive at an etrier, 'biner and piton that had been left behind at the same height as the eight-foot roof that juts out horizontally to my right. The rope angles up and right so I will have to execute what appears to be a very short pendulum. Another intriguing phenomenon on the north face of Windtower are the huge planes of rock at goofy angles. The whole wall overhangs, but large oblique portions of the wall tend to create illusions of where the vertical really is. The slope below the face also falls steeply away below, angling down and to the right. This too, contributes to the illusion. The upshot of all this is that the short pendulum to my right is actually much longer than I think it is.

The season of 1986 ended and the snow began to fly. Jeff and I hooked up in November for a drinking session. I recall we had to shut the party down and then continue to another informal gathering at a residence. We shut that follow-up party down, too, and were standing on the curb under lamplight just before heading our separate ways, when Jeff said, "You know Steve, sometimes you can be a bit pushy." I was taken aback and somewhat hurt by his comment. I found it hard to see how anyone could take my drive and enthusiasm as "pushy." I was so choked that I did not have a response.

Our second year on the wall in 1987 saw many attempts. On one of our efforts, Jeff aided up pitch 4. He made a horrendous string of body-weight placements, back-cleaning as he went. Wow! A true master — back-cleaning to save gear for higher up.

Now 20 feet out and hanging from yet another tied-off knife blade, he said: "Hmmm, thought I saw some dirt fall out of the crack. Naw, must've been light reflecting off my glasses from somewhere."

And then came the frightening "chink" of a piton ripping out of a crack.

"Oooh!"

The kid sailed for 40 feet and landed upside down beside me with a clatter of ironmongery.

"You OK son?"

"Uh … yeah."

Later that summer, Jeff was primed for the big push that I had been waiting for. I, though, was distracted with life and just couldn't get comfortable with the idea of going up on the wall. I couldn't explain it. It was almost like Windtower and I were two positively charged magnets. The more I wanted to get close to it, the greater was the force pushing me away. At the same time I was gripped that Jeff would bag the route without me.

The weathered piton creaks in an expanding flake. The frayed etrier is clipped to the pin with a retreats 'biner. I'm hanging in a familiar place on the wall, only it has been 15 years since I last touched these cracks. The piton and etrier are not from our ascent. On the surface it appears that another party had attempted the route, but had backed off. My jumars are both clipped onto the single lead line. The jug line angles out to my right at the lip of the sharp overhang. Raphael has done a fabulous lead on the pitch without any ado whatsoever. Eric is busy below, organizing gear to be hauled.

Yeah, I could clip the dead-line into this 'biner and lower myself out to the right, but it is such a short distance I might just as well use the etrier and let myself out slowly to the right. My legs are dangling in space while my nose is right at the height of the overhang. The lip has got a sharper edge to it than I remember. It doesn't occur to me to even attempt to remove the booty from the crack and add it to our rack.

Because I had keffled out, Jeff returned to the wall in August of '87 with Glenn Reisenhoffer. Glenn was extremely talented and had a cool head. A few years later he would become one of Canada's most versatile climbers on rock, ice and alpine ground; there would be virtually no kind of terrain that would stop him. At this point in his development, however, he was a keen newcomer to big wall tactics. The first fixed rope on Windtower would be his first time jumaring. For this reason, they decided not to freight-train with packs clipped to their harnesses, but rather have Glenn jumar the first rope and then haul up the bags. The first fixed rope hung below the eight-foot roof and for the first 80 feet Glenn dangled in space, spinning slowly around as he ascended. It was not easy, but Glenn did a fine job.

About 10 feet from the anchor at the top of the rope, Glenn noticed a tattered scrap of rope hanging down. His first thought was, "what the hell kind of rope work have these guys got up here?" His second thought was one of concern which evolved into real fear. Slowly, ever so slowly, he moved his jumars up enough to be able to grab the hanging end of tattered rope. Instinctively he tied a figure eight on a bight and clipped it into his harness. The sight that unfolded in front of him made his mouth go dry and his pupils dilate. On the two-bolt anchor that the fixed line had been clipped to, one of the carabiners had been smashed by rockfall so badly that it had fallen off the bolt and lay broken on the ledge. The remaining carabiner was intact, but the rope was cut 90 per cent through and only five strands remained. If only for a moment the seasoned rock climber felt vertigo. He had just jumared up the first 180 feet on these strands. Like a caterpillar, he even more carefully ascended the remaining few feet to the anchor. Jeff and particularly Glen were glad they had not freight-trained with the packs.

I use the etrier to lower myself to the right. Yes, this will work fine. Letting go of the etrier, I am surprised to find that I am in an accelerating pendulum swing further to the right. The rope is slicing along the lip of the roof at a great pace. I am 80 feet off the tarmac and my only thought is, "Jesus Christ, I'm a dad! I'm a dad!" At the same instant I throw my hand in between the rock and the rope, attempting to keep the rope off the sharp edge. But my feet are in space and it is impossible to create a gap. The back of my hand, while protecting my lifeline, slices along the lip of the overhang. My swing comes to a stop. The rope is intact. The skin on the back of my hand, though, looks like it has been buckshot. Ridges of skin stick out like tufts of pilling pile.

When Jeff told me what had happened, I was stone quiet for 15 minutes. I always jugged first. I was 30 pounds heavier than Glenn and would have freight-trained with a 50-pound pack clipped to me. Would that have tipped the scale? Somehow I had known about the rope. My instincts had screamed for me not to go on that attempt. I could not fathom it at the time and it was only in reflection that I realized my intuition had warned me. After that I listened more acutely to what these more subtle signals were telling me. If the desire and fire were not there, there must be a reason, even if it was not clear at the time. This was my first glaring incident regarding intuition.

I arrive at the belay where Raf and Eric are busy organizing gear. My hand is bloody and smarts. It looks as though it is merely a flesh wound and that no tendon damage has been done. The packs are a bitch to haul. Raf soon takes off on the next pitch, heading off toward the corner system out right. I begin helping Eric with the portaledge. Eventually it is set up correctly, but it becomes evident that there is not really a good spot for my old faithful hammock. Over the two hours at this belay, I begin developing irrational fears: The ropes are going to cut, the bolts are going to fail, huge flakes are going to peel off the face and crush us. There is no motivating and focusing tingle in my chest.

At the sight of blood, the warhorse, for the first time in many years, sees casualties parading back from the battlefield. In moments his breathing is constricted, and his nostrils flared as memories of pain and death come flooding back to him.

A week after Jeff and Glenn's return from the wall, I was ready for a fresh push. Without incident Jeff and I freight-trained to the high point. I left the belay feeling light and keen and scampered away like a mountain goat up into a corner capped by a large roof. The route finding was tricky because it was virtually impossible to see more than 60 or 70 feet at a time on this wall. (There was no good vantage point from which to view rock features from below and we did not have a photograph.) It appeared to make sense to traverse left under the roof. Pretty soon the footholds and handholds disappeared and I was forced to aid out left along a tight seam. The seam got tighter and tighter to the point where it would not even take the tip of my smallest blade. It was not hookable either. I spied a slight opening farther out, very shallow, about $3/16$ of an inch deep and $3/16$ of an inch wide. As I hung from my cow's tail and etriers, I stacked four of my pitons one on top of the other and tied them all together with cord. I held a fifth piton in my teeth while I gingerly placed the four in the slot. Then taking the piton from my teeth, I slid it in between the four pins with two on either side. Still holding them in place, I retrieved my hammer on its leash, and tap tap tapped in the fifth piton. I wrapped a tie-off around the whole shooting match as close as I could to the rock to minimize leverage, then clipped them all together into one 'biner, so that if they ripped they would not hurtle down the face. Five pins all at once would be a huge loss for us — we only had 15.

Next, I clipped an etrier onto the tie-off and hollered: "OK. Testing," in order to prepare Jeff in the event that my placement pulled. I clipped the rope into the piece I was on, then unclipped my cow's tail. If the stacked pins ripped, my prior piece, too, would easily pull if I shock-loaded it in a direct fall onto my cow's tail. I gently stepped onto the etrier. It held. I cleared my feet from my other etrier on the prior anchor as well before fully weighting my stacked pins. If the stacked pins failed and my foot was stuck in the prior etrier, I would be shot upside down, possibly whacking my head on the rock and wrenching my ankle. That would be bad.  It was important to go through the "what ifs" ritual piece by piece.

It seemed to be holding. And then with a clatter louder than dumping out your cutlery drawer onto concrete, I was dangling at the end of the rope 10 feet down. "Damn." The cluster of bread, butter and steak knives clinked at my waist.

*The Iron Butterfly leaps off the unstable limestone flower and flutters its wings in defiance. Though unfettered, it lands back on the fragile plant and continues its work.*

As it was a traverse, my lead line was up and to my right out of reach. I needed to jumar back up the rope to get back to the crack. I glanced back to my right at Jeff sitting at the belay. He was quiet save for a little twinkle in his eye. The edges of his pursed lips showed a slight curl upward at each end. He was having fun. I replied to his look with a loud "OOOOEEEE Son!" as I clipped my jumars onto the rope that held my fall and jugged back up to the anchor.

I repeated the process and wham! I fell and was again at the end of the rope.

I repeated the process a third time: Wham!

I repeated the process a fourth time. Again wham!

All of this had taken about an hour. After I had taken my fifth fall from the same place, I glanced back at Jeff: "It's a good thing it's me taking all these falls up here. Someone else might be shit scared!"

I escape to the scree below the face. A small bivy shelter has been built there at some time in the last 13 years. I settle in with my sleeping bag, some food and water. I have not bivied out in the open for perhaps 10 years. The mosquitoes arrive to take my thoughts away from the fact that come morning I am going to let the lads down. That is, retreat. I try to convince myself that they have the gear, food and water to continue. Nevertheless, I feel terrible about it. I remember it was always an extreme disappointment when a partner wasn't into it and you were.

The warhorse strains again on his bridle, but this time in the opposite direction, away from the front. Away from the fighting.

Jeff seconded the traverse. Seconding a traverse on aid is a tricky business at the best of times. It makes it simpler if you leave lots of gear behind, something that was not an option for us, and even if it was, it was something we both abhorred. Jeff was at the pendulum point, which was only slightly higher than where I had taken the belay. He managed to wedge himself across the overhanging slot where I had placed two wires in equal tension to pendulum from. The rock was steep and smooth here with very few holds. I was sure it would be high 5.12 if it were free climbed. Jeff unweighted the pieces and removed them. He was smeared out on the tiniest of edges, the wall scooped in below him. With a sudden realization, he looked over at me, down 10 feet to the next piece and then back to me. We both knew it was too late for him to attempt to wiggle the wires back in from his precarious and strenuous perch. With a grimace he grunted, "This is really stupid" and without even a hint of a rattle, he let go — completely in control — and took a 20-foot fall onto the anchor below.

One of the neat things about the north wall of Windtower is that once above the ledge at the top of pitch 2, there is not a ledge even big enough to set a water bottle on for a 1000 feet. And though the climbing is hard, it's actually quite safe by relative standards, because if you do take a fall you will rarely hit anything.

*A wing is torn and dented slightly on the Butterfly's metal body. Blood has been let. It leaves a scar, but heals well. The education is worth it.*

When pitches take four or five hours to lead, you are on the wall for a least a few days in order to climb it. Of course, this presents some accommodation issues. I was quietly sleeping in my hammock when I awoke at 3:30 a.m. realizing I had to urinate bad. I had forgotten to bring a pee bottle. It was very dark. I managed to work my way out of my sleeping bag and claw my way up on one of my etriers. I struggled to stay in balance, one foot insecurely in my hammock, the other swinging uncontrollably in the etrier. My right hand had a death grip on the top rung of my etrier, the left fought feverishly with my harness and pile pants. It was here where I received my biggest pump on the route: Hanging there, poised in the wind for 60 seconds, relieving my overloaded bladder.

The morning arrives. I have had a terrible night. Mostly beating myself up for letting Raf and Eric down. I give them the news first thing. I know they are not impressed, but they hide their extreme disappointment well. I am going down. Once the news is out, I just want to get away from this arena. I no longer belong to this place. Hiking out, there are a few tricky bits around some small rock bands. It occurs to me that I am even gripped on the approach trail.

The old warhorse, finally free of his ropes, limps back from the front, his eyes glazed with memory, his heart pounding with anticipation of the future, yet forlorn at a loss that he cannot yet understand.

During another five-hour lead, I dosed off during a sugar crash after consuming all of a big bag of peanut M&Ms. Through my dreams echoed Jeff's voice, "I'm in trouble."

From within my narrow and unconscious world I heard more the strain in his voice than understood the meaning of his words. I had been feeding the rope out a foot at a time for the last two and a half hours. My lips repeated Jeff's words and vaguely I became aware of the implication of his remark. Out of the dream world my mind stumbled. I was falling, tumbling, straining. My vision was blurred in a blinding sun, my limbs moved only in slow motion. My teeth ground in frustration as my jaws clamped tighter and tighter. Blood drained from my gums and uncontrollably the force on my teeth amplified until they began to crumble and snap. My mouth was filled with tooth splinters. I hissed in rage and blew phlegm and broken teeth through blood-drenched lips. My conscious mind screamed "IT'S ONLY A DREAM!" Finally, my eyes shot open and I plummeted into the conscious world. Suddenly I could move. I jolted back onto the belay slings and struggled, squirming in my harness, to see over the rock bulge just above me and into the groove beyond. My free hand unconsciously stuffed fingers into my mouth to check my incisors and molars. They were intact.

The groove, more like a scoop actually, featured a concave slab at its base with a more savagely concave ceiling above. Jeff was spread-eagled across this undercut ceiling, his legs almost horizontal, his feet smeared on tiny edges. Jeff's torso, twisted fiercely to the right, seemed only to be held in place by a small side-cling placed rather inconveniently at the end of his outstretched left arm. I could see his last piece, a bolt drilled from a sky-hook, situated 20 feet below and close to the centre of the scoop. I immediately understood the gravity of his words. If Jeff blew off, he would drop into the bottom of the scoop. His legs would snap like dry matchsticks.

Both Jeff and I understood the seriousness of our position on the wall that overhung for over a thousand feet. Retreat with one of us injured would not be an easy task. I had been able to witness Jeff in many very extreme climbing situations over the two years I had climbed with him and I had never heard him make any such proclamation.

"James!?" I hail.

Some might consider my hail an unfit interruption for Jeff who was on lead and obviously in some state of concern. The nature of our partnership, however, had matured from a sheepish East meets West introduction into one where we both felt comfortable disclosing our individual quirks and weaknesses on and off the rock. This was very special to me; there was no competition between us, only a mutual respect for one another's abilities and limitations. As we ventured from steep limestone wall to steep limestone wall in the Bow Valley, this respect grew into a peculiar kind of loyalty to each other and our cause. Our almost caring nature for each other was such that when either of us was on a hard lead, we welcomed a second viewpoint from the belay. It helped us to get the big picture. In this case though, my suggestion seemed merely a reiteration of the obvious:

"That is not a good place to fall!"

Jeff, even under the strain and seriousness of his position, answered almost as though we were having an intellectual conversation at a coffee shop: "I know."

That was all that had to be said. Both Jeff and I understood the nature of the game. It was part of the allure: The focus, the accuracy and the control. We joyed in the strife of championing these pitches, of mastering poise in the face of poor protection and suspect rock, not because we were crazy, but because we wanted to deal with these situations. We wanted to test ourselves, to see if our creative and analytical minds could piece together a route up this wall, a route that could be climbed not only safely, but also in complete control.

Jeff's answer "I know" was indicative of this poise. Calmness in the face of extreme physical and mental stress allowed him to remain controlled enough to further assess his position. I watched, this time grinding my teeth consciously, as Jeff dipped into his chalk bag. I heard his deep controlled breaths. He adjusted his left foot, moving it to another small nubbin of rock slightly higher. First he tapped the nubbin gently with his toe to feel and listen for the invisible fracture which would render the foothold off limits. Then he gingerly placed his foot on the rugosity. He laid back on his extended left hand — his right did not appear to have a hold of much of anything — then took his right foot from the rock. I cringed. This I knew was a very strenuous position. His right arm began a gentle arc towards what seemed a blank section of rock. But as I watched I saw his fingers disappear into a hidden edge. Jeff's feet pranced easily up to another set of slopers, his breathing suggesting that everything, at least for now, was cool. I sank back onto the slings when I heard the tap tap tap of a bolt being drilled.

*The Iron Butterfly knows fear, but now embraces it as a tool. Even a slight vibration gives an early warning of danger. In this, it has a new confidence.*

A few weeks later I find out that Jeff was on the north east face of Windtower on the same day and night. The north east face is around a large buttress from the north west face, so it is not possible for climbers to see each other. Neither Jeff nor I had been back for 13 years since our ascent and then, unknowingly, we both approach and bivy on the mountain on the same night.

On the morning of day three we woke up to a snowstorm and a sharp temperature drop. We knew this was our last chance on the wall that year.

"What would George Lowe do if he was in this position?"

I decided to go rub my nose in the next pitch to really get a feel for just how cold it was. I had all my clothes and wind gear on, but as I aided up, my feet were freezing and my hands were cold. We had carried only three litres of water each up the route, expecting to take three days. We did not have the provisions to wait out bad weather. Jeff and I commenced our retreat.

On June 20 of the following year, 1988, Jeff and I again arrived at the col. This was our first view of the wall up close in nine months. This time we had all of the toys to go for a final assault. We were silent as we started up the first talus above the col. As we approached the face across the scree, Jeff asked, "How do you feel?"

"Like Clint Eastwood going into a gunfight." And I exaggerated my gait over the scree one well-placed foot at a time. "I'm cool, focused and ready to respond to whatever comes our way." Jeff didn't have to make eye contact with me to know that I wasn't being melodramatic.

We arrived at the ropes. They had been left untouched for nine months through a Rockies winter.

"Well, there are no ropes lying on the scree. That's a start."

After Glenn's incident we were concerned about the ropes. Conventional jumaring technique has one hanging solely from the mechanical clamps of the jumars. Only these clamps and the rope keep you off the deck. There is really no back up. It is simple: If one jumars the ropes in conventional style and a fixed rope snaps someone will be dead. Carrying a 50 pound pack clipped to a harness is hard work, but significantly faster than hauling. It is called "freight training." This extra weight on the winterized ropes is an additional factor.

Jeff and I had been stormed off so many times that neither of us wanted to risk being on the wall one more day than necessary. Belaying would add an extra day to our climb.

Then I had an idea that I explained to Jeff: "We will uncoil our two climbing ropes and both of us tie in at each end as we normally do were climbing. I will jumar the first rope. This will be the most dangerous rope of all — 800 feet of fixed line. Once at the first anchor I will clip a draw into the anchor bolt and then continue on the next fixed line. You will start to jumar on the first rope once I am on the second. If the rope I am on snaps, I will have a running belay from you as we simultaneously jumar our respective ropes. The worst-case scenario will be a 300-foot fall, but at least it would be into space. That is, an air fall. It would at least give us a chance of survival." Jeff liked the plan. He also liked the fact that I would be jumaring out front on the first rope.

As we ascended, I felt quite safe. At some points we had more than one bolt clipped between us. This felt like a luxury. The fixed lines were in good shape. Unbelievably good shape, in fact. It was like they had been fixed the week before. After the Glenn episode we had expected to re-lead the odd pitch because a weathered fixed line had chaffed through, but this was not the case. To us it was like a miracle. Even the very last rope, an 8 mm, which I jumared with a proper belay, was in remarkably good condition.

*The Iron Butterfly darts in and out from the wall at will. Bits of iron adhere to tiny cracks and rugosities in the limestone flower. It is with the pleasure of an artist, the precision of a surgeon and the aggressiveness of an attack helicopter that the insect toils away at its masterpiece, ever aware of the fragility and delicate nature of its existence and survival in this place.*

I hitch a ride back into Canmore and make my way to the house we have rented for our holiday. I am walking down the street feeling sorry for myself, when who happens to be driving by in their car but

Choc Quinn, Chris Perry and Chas Yonge on their way to go cragging. Of course, I'm carrying a big pack and it's only about 8:30 a.m.

They see me and pull over, "Where are you going?"

I'm caught. Damn! If I'd at least recognized the vehicle, I could have made an attempt to hide in the bushes. I won't be able to stick-handle out of this one.

"Well ... " I begin, and quickly tell them all about my shortcomings.

I reached the top of the fixed lines and began an improbable rising traverse up and to the right on pitch 8. I doweled and hooked across the blank section, leaving a hook on an edge 10 inches down and to the left, held on in quasi-tension from the rope. The hook I was on blew. I sailed through space until the rope came tight with hardly a tug at my waist. I looked above and was immediately awed.

"Holy shit!"

"What?"

"The hook held!"

I swung over and grabbed the rope that ran up to the hook.

"Elevator going up!"

"What!? You're not going to haul yourself back up on the hook are you?"

"It held the fall didn't it?"

The rock beyond was too rotten to hold hooks and there were no cracks. I needed to get over to the right about 20 feet. I could not pendulum because the wall was overhanging and I'd just be dangling in space. And I didn't want to drill a bolt ladder because it would take too long and use up our limited supply of bolts. I tried drilling a bat hole to hook on, but the edge of the hole crumbled under my weight when I attempted to hook it. So I invented a dowelling technique. I drilled a hole about $3/8$ to $1/2$ of an inch deep on a slight downward angle, inserted the shaft of a bolt into this hole and then tied off the shaft with a very light shoe-lace cord. When I weighted the cord, the bolt shaft wedged into the hole and distributed the force over a much larger area than the hook did. It worked; the rock did not crumble. Jeff was impressed with my creativity in the moment.

As I continued to dowel across the blank section, I yelled down to Jeff, "I'm probably going to get shit for drilling holes like this 50 years from now."

There had just been a philosophical battle in Grotto Canyon after the "Banff Guys" had drilled handholds in an overhanging wall to create a route hard enough for them to climb. (I didn't quite understand the logic.) The whole episode had culminated in fixed ropes and a gas-fired Honda generator being stolen from their construction projects in the canyon. Of course, Jeff was blamed as the culprit and had been surrounded at his place of employment, then the MEC, by a group of "Banff Guys" and threatened. Though he agreed with the group that had taken the ropes, Jeff had not had anything to do with the incident.

This was only part of the tension between Calgary and Banff at the time. Jeff and I liked to climb big routes. We used bolts only as a last resort for pro. Our routes were in the mid 5.11 range, considered in 1986 and '87 a solid standard to climb in traditional ground up style, particularly on Rockies limestone. It was suggested by the "Banff Guys" that there was no way it was possible we could climb that hard up high with such a minimal amount of gear, on limestone and on new ground. And even if we could, it was only because we had a death wish and were glory hungry. All this culminated in the "Banff Kids" completing the second ascent of one of our climbs, Astro Yam, and claiming, as the five of them surrounded Jeff at MEC, that it was only 5.10. This had all taken place only a few months before. I was pissed: "Too bad they didn't surround ME at my place of employment!" I was a much larger lad than Jeff and probably meaner.

It all gave me a bad taste in my mouth. So to make my own little statement, I did not take a camera on our final assault on Windtower — something I deeply regret today. This I felt would prove I was not glory hungry. There was such tension between the two camps that Jeff and I had half expected to find our fixed ropes chopped or removed from Windtower when we returned. Of course, when they were still there, we both muttered something sarcastic and scathing about crag fags being too scared even to jumar our ropes.

Choc, Chris and Chas are quite sympathetic to my story and invite me to go sport climbing for the day. For a moment I consider accepting, but then look at my hand. It is oozing a bloody pus and still smarts. I can't imagine another four days on the wall with my hand in such a condition. Chalk (or salt) in my wounds all day is not a real appetizing prospect. Plus I just want to be alone in my misery.

Jeff began cleaning the pitch and I began the process of hauling. Both packs were clipped into the haul line. The haul line was clipped into a piece at the far end of the 30-foot rising traverse. Jeff was wrestling with the packs, attempting to unclip the haul line from the 'biner, when the piece pulled and both Jeff and the packs flew across the wall. Then the dowels ripped out of the traverse and all three of them sailed into space. I got flashed a rare look of terror:

"You OK son?"

"Ow! Ow! Ow! ... Rope burn! Rope burn!"

By the time Jeff and the packs reached the station it was more or less time to rig up our hammocks. The night passed uneventfully and in the morning it was Jeff's lead. We were high on the wall. It would be tricky to get back to our fixed lines at the other end of the A4 traverse in a retreat. We packed up everything except for my hammock. "Hmmm, might as well just belay out of the hammock. It is likely to be a three to five hour lead and any fool can be uncomfortable!"

Belaying out of my hammock had its own other associated benefits. It made it easier to become hypnotized by the whisper of the thermals as they swept down over the vast expanse of this cool north wall. It also facilitated being caressed to sleep by the cadence of a hammer tap tap tapping in a piton or drilling a bolt. This dream world provided a brief respite from the stress of our labours and position.

The warhorse returns to the pasture, the plough, his farm, his labours, his offspring and is grateful for his station. A colt cavorts in the long grass next to the barn. It whinnies a greeting as the old stallion limps onto the property. The mare had sensed him coming from over a mile away. She makes eye contact with him briefly and then continues to scrape and stamp the straw into the dirt with her hooves, but with slightly less vigor.

When I arrive at our residence, I shower, shave and re-dress the abrasions and cuts on my hand. I stare down at my two rings sitting on the bathroom countertop. I grasp my wedding band and slide it on my finger. I feel a tingling in my chest and close my eyes.

Visions of our little family flash on the backs of my eyelids. Stephanie is playing in the sprinkler. Karen is tossing a salad behind the counter in the kitchen, but is watching Stephie through the window. She is glowing and her eyes sparkle. Is this why I came down? Or is it less complex? Risk/Reward? I have already climbed the north west face of Windtower and because of that fact the reward is less. This is called "Marginal Utility" in economic theory. And because I haven't climbed much, am out of shape — both mentally and physically — the risks are also higher. In the business world, a higher risk for less reward is not a good use of investment capital. Then I pick up the stainless steel ring of my professional designation. It is only six months ago that I completed the fund-raising endeavour for Efficient. I had made serious commitments to those people too. The new dressing on the back of my hand stings from the peroxide. Or is it merely that my cup is overfull right now.

Jugging the pitch brought us into the upper corner. For the first time in 1000 feet of climbing the wall did not overhang. I sorted the rack quickly and began the next lead. The corner was running with water for about 50 feet above. However, I spied another crack system out right. This one took me to a small ledge about four inches wide. This is the first ledge big enough to place a water bottle on since the top of pitch 2. I was out of sight from Jeff so I hailed him "James?"

"Yo!?"

"It's getting dark. I don't think we should go for the top. I don't want to fuck around when we are so close. It's only another 80 feet and we'll have plenty of time in the morning."

We set up hammocks for our last hours on the wall. I awoke to the warmth of sunlight on my face. I shut my eyes and tried to absorb as much of it as I could. It was only the second time in three years that I had felt the sun's rays on this wall. The cloud level was 500 feet below us … we could be millions of miles away on another planet. I could hardly believe that tomorrow I would be back at work, standing again atop scaffolding tacking up aluminium soffit and siding. We would top out this morning, I knew we would, but strangely I could not focus on the summit. Rather I stared down the steep walls of the upper dihedral into the clouds.

I had climbed Windtower in my other life, a life where I was a tough and seasoned climber, a warhorse in his prime. I was meant to be there and meant to manage those risks. I had evolved inside my cocoon, developing as a climber, and ultimately had had the confidence to slice it open and emerge as an "Iron Butterfly" — tough, yet delicate enough to climb in that serious place in a controlled and safe manner. To go back and drink again the nectar from that limestone flower was not to be. Things are different. I am different. My life and expectations are different. My responsibilities have evolved. It is not just me any more. There is our little family and my professional obligations. Both will suffer if I neglect the other. Retreat or failure in either case will leave a trail of carnage more painful than Raf or Eric's disappointment in my retreat. This is not a good place to fall.

> We had spent so much time on this wall. Between us we'd felt the joys of leading intricate and dangerous pitches, felt the fear of falling from winterized ropes, felt anger at the weather conditions, felt frustration at our pace and, finally, felt anxiety when we left the fixed lines and knew we had no choice but to continue upwards. I looked back up the last 80 feet. Why did I feel like we should rap back down, when yesterday from 300 feet lower down I'd not have given an inch?
>
> Jeff and I topped off without any further incident, shouldered our much lighter loads and began our decent down the backside of the mountain.
>
> "James, do you remember that conversation we had a few years back when I said that you were too pushy?"
>
> "Yeah." I responded. Of course I remembered. I had never forgot.
>
> "Yeah well … that's one of the things I like the best about you." We both laughed like children, howled, shook hands and continued our descent.

*The Butterfly flits and floats gleefully in the turbid air as it rotors over the twin-peaked summit. It makes its way back down to the valley playfully, making random turns and loop-the-loops as though drunk in delight with its newfound confidence and strength. There is a reaffirmed passion that only ignites in the atmosphere of naivete. In the short life of an insect, though, it never seems to last long enough. And is gone before it is really understood or appreciated.*

Six weeks after our ascent of Windtower, Brian Wallace was killed on our attempt to climb the north face of Mount Lougheed. I was seriously shaken, my confidence rattled. I had planned to return to university prior to the accident, so a hiatus from climbing to focus on this other objective was already in the works. I continued to try to make sense of the accident and the guilt of my own survival. I begin drafting an expression of my thoughts on risk in an article entitled *The Psycho/Physical Edge.*

Andy Genereux, Jeff and I returned to the wall five weeks later and completed the route. We named it "The Warrior" in Brian's honour. The next day I attended my first classes at the University of Calgary. Sitting in a lecture hall, I felt out of place and could not relate to the other students. I was also feeling guilty about the good feelings I had about completing our project on Windtower. Jeff and I had pulled it off. I believed that we had managed the risks with skill and were very much in control the whole time. I also relived again and again the series of decisions that were made leading up to Brian's fatal fall on Loughheed. In my heart I was convinced that his death could have been avoided.

When I head back to the office, there is only a passing acknowledgement by my staff that I am back early. The chairman of the board suggests I have been negligent for even having made an attempt at Windtower. When the board insured the company with Key-Man Insurance they had decided not to pay the extra few thousand dollars per year for coverage while I was climbing.

In hindsight, I can see that my whole climbing paradigm changed after Brian was killed. I became much more conservative. I started to get scared. Up to that point I had not backed off a limestone lead in four years. The years that followed saw me back off many routes, as well as turn around at the base of many climbs just because I didn't feel right. I also did not have the same passion for dangerous ground. It got to the point where intricate and serious pitches became just something to get through.

It was similar to what happened when I played high school football. At the time I was getting very serious about my climbing and had begun to realize that I was letting up on the field because I grew fearful of destroying a knee which would affect my climbing career: It was then that I was in the greatest danger of getting hurt, when I could no longer give 120 per cent because of that fear. I quit the football team and began focusing on climbing. I was 17 years old.

By the end of 2003 I reflect that I may be retired for good from serious climbing. Periodically my brain floats to various unfinished climbing goals and my heart quickens. I feel a tingle in my chest. The warhorse in me stamps his hooves, whips his head up and down making his main fly and snorts with excitement. But then my hands go to the fleshy tire around my middle.

I feel a tug on my pant leg. "Daddy, what are we going to do now?" A five month old is cooing and making sucking noises in the background. "Mommy and Daddy are going to the indoor climbing gym this afternoon."

A few weeks later a seasoned businessman and shareholder of Efficient Energy approaches me at a Christmas party: "I'm real pleased Steve. You pulled it out of the fire after last year. When I invested I said, 'We are investing in the management team.' Everyone who knew you said, 'Steve is a pit-bull.' But what I really want to know is, how are you? Personally? Are you achieving balance in your life? You are no good to yourself, your family or the corporation if you auger yourself into the ground."

I stare off into space for an instant. My vision blurs and I can hear my hammer and feel the vibration in my hand as I tap tap tap in a knife blade, coercing it into a tight but expanding seam. There is loose rock all around me. I have been climbing on eggshells above a ledge for 50 feet. This is not a good place to fall.

In December of 2004, while in that "no fall situation," Efficient Energy takes a long factor II fall onto the belay. Five pieces in the station rip out. This leaves me and all the stakeholders hanging by only a small micro wire out over the abyss. I am badly injured, having come very close to augering in. For a year I'd hung by my fingernails trying to manage the business and operating risks in a paradigm of diminishing resources. My fingers are bloody where my nails have scraped stone for too long. After four years on this expedition I am tired. I had considered jumping off several times to end the suffering, but my core fibres would not allow it. Finally, a large stonefall knocks the corporation off the rock surface. In the subsequent fall onto the belay, one lead line is cut clean through. The other has only five small white strands remaining.

I bump into the same shareholder at the same party a long tough year since we had last talked. He has been receiving regular quarterly updates. "Well Steve, no one likes to lose money. You've put your shoulder into it and none of us could have asked for any more than that. Don't fall on your sword over it. We are all big boys here and we knew the risks going in."

I am still choked that I could not force a way through to the top before the objective and subjective hazards wiped us out. Neither rapping off nor leaving fixed ropes is an option. I've seen the good and the bad in people facing tough situations, discomfort, ambiguity and risk over the last few years. The fight is not yet done. As yet I have not had any time to reflect on all the lessons I have learned. The costs, financially and emotionally, have been great. The reward? Perhaps only the education. Other "climbers" suggest I'll bounce back quickly, but it's not clear whether I will be craving these heights anytime soon.

That said, as of the winter 2005, Raf and Eric have never gone back and the other line on Windtower remains unfinished.

In my dreams I may climb it.

The rock is steep
and way too smooth.

3 a.m. the crux.
I am struggling to stay
in balance, one foot
securely in the hammock,
the other swinging
uncontrollably in the etrier.
My right hand a death grip
on the top rung, the left
fighting furiously
with my harness and pants.
Hanging there,  poised in the wind
I relieve my overloaded bladder.

"I'm in trouble."
I start and strain to see above.
"James?" a grunt.
He's above a ramp.
I cringe.
That's not a good place to fall."
"I know."

## Kids on the Wind

Jeff wedges himself across a savage slot
With a grimace he grunts
"This is really stupid"
and calmly lets go
and hurtles twenty feet.

Crappy stacked pins
rattle in the seam.
Tap tap tap.
They hold my weight.
Then comes a clatter
like a cutlery drawer being
dumped on a concrete floor
as I take to the air,
then jerk and hang
again from my rope.
Carefully I re-place
my knife blades and arrows.
Tap tap tap.
They rip again
and I plummet
FIVE MORE TIMES
from the same place.
Good thing it's me
taking all these falls.
Someone else might be shit scared!

# Escalating Commitment

On the headwall
  there is no pro.
  I have banged in
    five anchors below.
    Surely
      one of them will hold?
      I power through
        the bulge.
        Am established
          on the headwall.
          But I'm pumped.
          Downclimb!
            DOWNCLIMB!
          Coming off!
            Fifteen-foot fall.
            OK!
              I can do this.
              Rock & Roll man.
              I sift past the holds
                in a trance
                to a new high point.
                FUCK!
                No jam left.
                  Twenty-five foot fall.
                  One piton pulled half out
                  I bang it back in.
                  Good rest.
                  OK!
                    Watch me this time.
                    I'm going for it.
                    I hesitate …
                      one foot higher
                      FFUUCCKK!
                        Thirty-five foot fall.

Now I'm pissed.
 OK man
  This is it!
   I bolt through the crux.
    I'm five feet from the top
     on easy ground
      but my fingers are opening.
       My legs churn
        like a paddle wheel.
         FFFUUUCCCKKK!
          I'm gripped about decking
           OK man!
            I'm coming off!
             Take it in.
              TAKE IT RIGHT FUCKING IN!
              PULL ME OFF!
               An unfamiliar
                downward force
                 on my harness
                  FFFFUUUUCCCCKKKK!
                   Fifty-five foot fall.

                   My belayer
                    sees a snake
                     coil on the ground beside him
                      and then disappear.
                       He is launched
                        but keeps the rope locked.
                         That's the furthest fucking fall
                          he has ever seen.

# Glossary

*aid, aid climbing:* 1) To make progress up a rock face solely facilitated by the use of etriers and the of placing anchors or other ironmongery in cracks or on edges of the rock. 2) The use of such techniques. Antonym: Free climbing.

*air fall:* A leader fall where the climber does not hit anything on the way down so the rope absorbs all the energy of the fall (as opposed to various body parts absorbing the forces of impact). Usually on vertical or overhanging ground. Often quite safe to take. Antonym: A no-fall situation.

*anchor:* Usually two or more pieces of protection placed at a belay or a rappel station. Often all tied together with the climbing rope or with an independent short piece of cord. Can be used to describe a running belay or an individual piece of protection that the climber has clipped the rope into whilst on lead. The rope slides freely through this anchor point.

*Bachar ladder:* A rope ladder with wooden or rope rungs. When hung from a tree or other structure at an angle, it is climbed with arms only for upper body training.

*Bat-hole:* A shallow hole drilled in the rock for up to 5 mm solely for the purpose of placing a sky-hook while on aid. Used on otherwise blank rock instead of drilling a medium-depth hole for a dowel or rivet, or a full-depth hole for a bolt.

*belay:* n. The place at which the climber anchors himself at the beginning and end of a pitch. v. The act of holding the rope, usually through some form of friction device, for the purpose of safeguarding your climbing partner or partners.

*body-weight pieces:* Protection placements that will hold body weight, but not the full force of a fall from any great distance.

*bolt:* An anchor which requires the climber to first drill a hole in the rock and then place a steel shaft with a threaded end in the hole. A hanger is attached to the shaft with a nut or cap-screw. In traditional climbing they are used when there are no other alternatives for protection and where the climbing so severe that to climb without a bolt would be extremely dangerous.

*bolt kit:* The bolt driver and bit (the drill), bolts, hangers, capscrews, wrench, all in a small nylon bag.

*carabiner:* An alloy steel spring loaded snap-link which allows the rope or other climbing paraphernalia to be clipped to each other and/or the climber.

*chalk:* A powder of magnesium carbonate use on the climber's hands that helps keep them dry so they slip less on the rock surface.

*chalk bag:* A small nylon bag which holds the chalk, worn in a convenient location by the climber.

*cow's tail:* A short nylon sling with pre-made loops for adjusting length which is attached to the climber's harness. Used with carabiners to clip into aid placements or belay anchors.

*dihedral:* A rock formation which features two vertical and planar rock surfaces meeting at an oblique angle. Also known as a 'corner' or an 'open book.'

*dowel, to:* To drill a shallow hole and place a steel shaft in the hole to create a body-weight placement. The hole is usually drilled deeper than a bat-hole but shallower than for a bolt.

*etriers:* Used for aid climbing. They are short ladders made of nylon sling material that allow the climber to climb high on an aid placement in order to place another as high as possible. Also known as aiders.

*fixed line:* A climbing rope that has been left in place anchored to the rock.

*freight-train, to:* To ascend a fixed rope with jumars while hauling a 20 kg plus pack that dangles from your cow's tail while you ascend.

*Friend:* A protection device featuring a spring-loaded cam. Particularly good for use in parallel cracks.

*gently-impending:* Slightly overhanging. Just over-vertical.

*hang-dog:* To hang from the climbing rope or your cow's tail on a piece or pieces of protection repeatedly while climbing a pitch normally climbed without such tactics. May refer to attempts to free a pitch.

*hard-clip:* To clip the climbing harness directly into a piece of protection with a sling and two carabiners.

*harness:* Pre-made, adjustable webbing loops that are worn around the waist and legs. Typically features two loops in which to attach the climbing rope. Designed to distribute the forces of a fall across the buttocks and waist.

*hook:* n. A small J-shaped steel device for placing on edges of rock or in bat-holes. It looks like a beefy fish-hook but without the barb. They come in several sizes. v. To place the steel hook on a rock ledge.

*jug:* 1) A large in-cut hand-hold that inspires confidence. Aka. a thank-god hold. 2) to ascend a fixed rope with mechanical clamps called jumars. 3) A mechanical clamp or jumar.

*jugging:* The act of ascending a fixed rope with mechanical clamps.

*Jumars:* Mechanical clamps used for ascending fixed ropes.

*knife blade:* A thin piton.

*finger-lock:* 1) Crack climbing technique which features wedging one or more fingers in a thin tapering crack. 2) The place where a thin crack tapers.

*finger jam:* Same as finger lock.

*mantle:* A climbing maneuver which features a ledge over the head, but no foot holds. One must pull with the arms until enough height is gained to then rotate the palms downward and then push until the waist is even with the ledge. A foot is then raised onto the ledge to facilitate standing up on it.

*meat-hooks:* A climber's hands. Term used when a climber feels strong and confident.

*nut:* A small alloy steel wedge swaged on an steel cable that is used for protection. Term comes from the climbing pioneers who used industrial steel nuts they found on the railroad tracks and threaded them with a short cord. Also known as wires or stoppers.

*pendulum:* To swing on the climbing rope from an anchor. May be used to bypass a blank section of rock or it may occur if a fall is taken while out to the side of the nearest piece of protection.

*piece:* A running belay, a protection point.

*pin:* A metal spike that is driven into cracks or holes in the rock for protection and/or belays *piton:* Same as pin.

*portaledge:* A small, collapsible cot made from nylon and aluminum. Used for sleeping on rock-faces where there are no ledges.

*pumped:* When the fingers/hands are extremely fatigued and the forearms engorged with blood.

*rap/rappel:* To descend a rope or ropes usually using some type of friction device attached to the climbing harness.

*running belay:* A protection point that is clipped into the climbing rope with a carabiner so that the rope can slide through it as the climber continues up. Generally, a pitch will have 10 or 15 of these protection points — more or less —if the climbing is difficult or easy.

*screamer:* A leader fall of such length that you have time to scream. Generally 15 metres or more.

*side-cling:* A type of handhold, vertical in orientation, large enough only for the finger-tips. The climber must lay away to the left or right of it in order to maintain any purchase at all.

*sky-hook:* Same as hook.

*sling:* Nylon tape or webbing used for a variety of purposes, namely connecting the climber rope via a carabiner to an anchor point or piece of protection.

*slopers:* Sloping hand or footholds

*slot:* A niche, tight open book or short narrow chimney often with no bottom.

*smear, to:* To splay the bottom of a subtle climbing shoe over the rock in order to gain purchase on smooth, small or rounded surfaces or footholds.
Antonym: Edging.

*stitch plate:* A friction device that the rope is passed through. Used for belaying or rappelling.

*stopper:* Same as nut.

*wire:* Same as nut.

# Acknowledgments

Over the years there have been many people who have helped me in my writing endeavours. I would like to thank the following individuals for their investment of time and effort.

It was John Kaandorp who first introduced me to the concept of "shit-detector" and then helped me develop it. Always a good source of editorial feedback and insight, John in particular gave me extensive suggestions on early poetry and on the initial drafts of *The Psycho/Physical Edge* and *Jimmy and the Kid*. At the time, The P/P E was my most complex essay and John helped me focus my thoughts to make the narrative more clear.

Kari Strut, who taught me to "show" as opposed to "tell," worked with me on early poetry, on preliminary versions of *The Psycho/Physical Edge*, and completed both the early and final edits on the published version of *Jimmy and the Kid*. She, as did John, spent many hours carefully reading my material and then giving me verbal and written feedback. In fact, as I hand-wrote everything in those days, Kari even typed *Jimmy and the Kid* and printed it out on fine paper for its ultimate submission to the *CAJ*.

David Harris and Geoff Powter, in their respective roles as editors of the *Canadian Alpine Journal*, worked hard to make my writing stronger and tighter. I would also like to thank them for allowing me to experience the writer's high you get when your work finally comes out in print. Thank you both!

Bill Betts has always been a champion of mine on the rock, on paper and in life. His writing can be seen in his reflections in the essay, *The East End Boys*. Bill, I remain grateful for your continual mentorship.

Karen Snyder, now my wife, continues to give me feedback on my writing (among other things!). Specifically, she had several editorial suggestions on *The East End Boys* and *Surfin' the Curve*. Michelle Fleming and Jason de Jong also had significant influence on early versions of *Surfin' the Curve*. Jason also did the graphics for "The Curve" in *Surfin' the Curve*.

Chic Scott graciously accepted my invitation to write the foreword for this book, and once again exemplified his ability to cut to the marrow of a theme. He, too, has always been a champion of mine, and I am grateful for his support and understanding through the years.

Will Gadd and Mark Twight were very kind to read the book and to provide quotes for Rocky Mountain Book's marketing directives.

Gerry De Maio, my devoted and supportive brother, let me reproduce part of a letter he wrote to me in 1988 for *The Psycho/Physical Edge*. He also allowed us access to several of his photographs.

Thomas Walker graciously allowed us to re-publish one of his photographs for the cover of this book.

Gillean Daffern of Rocky Mountain Books remains an icon of enthusiasm, support and feedback for my stories, and for this book. She inspired me to attempt some new styles of poetry and challenged me on several of my existing works. Gill also identified the key theme for the book, along with the areas that needed improvement. It was a great source of joy for me to work with Gill who ultimately became more intimate with my stories than anyone else on the planet. I have very much enjoyed and appreciated the direction and feedback that she provided. Thank you Gillean.

## About the Author

Steve De Maio has been a risk taker for most of his life, exhibiting an early penchant for tree-climbing, aerial-rope and bike stunts before the age of ten. He began rock climbing at age 14 and since then has made over 150 first ascents in North America, some of which have never been repeated.

Steve lives in Calgary with his wife Karen and two children. When not working as a consultant in the energy industry, he pursues his passion for climbing, roller blading and martial arts. As a writer, he has won numerous awards for magazine articles and is currently working on his second book, a novel based on his work and climbing experiences.